WHAT COULD A UNIVERSITY BE?

UBC PRESS

The **On Campus** imprint of UBC Press features publications designed for the diverse members of the university community – students, faculty, instructors, staff, and administrators. **On Campus** offers a range of interesting, sometimes unconventional, but always useful information. All **On Campus** works are assessed by experts in the field prior to publication. To ensure affordability, PDFs are available as free downloads from the UBC Press website, with print and other digital formats also available through our website, bookstores, and libraries.

On Campus books are designed to help readers successfully meet the intellectual and social challenges encountered at university or college today and include:

How to Succeed at University (and Get a Great Job!): Mastering the Critical Skills You Need for School, Work, and Life, by Thomas R. Klassen and John A. Dwyer (also available in French from University of Ottawa Press)

It's All Good (Unless It's Not): Mental Health Tips and Self-Care Strategies for Your Undergrad Years, by Nicole Malette

You @ the U: A Guided Tour through Your First Year of University, by Janet Miller

The Successful TA: A Practical Approach to Effective Teaching, by Kathy M. Nomme and Carol Pollock

TL;DR: A Very Brief Guide to Reading and Writing in University, by Joel Heng Hartse

The Deliberate Doctorate: A Values-Focused Journey to Your PhD, by Leela Viswanathan

To find out more about **On Campus** books, visit www.ubcpress.ca or follow us on social media.

Robert Gibbs

What Could a University Be?

REVOLUTIONARY IDEAS FOR THE FUTURE

UBC PRESS

© 2025 On Campus, an imprint of UBC Press

All rights reserved. No part of this publication may be reproduced, stored in a retrieval system, or transmitted, in any form or by any means, without prior written permission of the publisher, or, in Canada, in the case of photocopying or other reprographic copying, a licence from Access Copyright, www.accesscopyright.ca.

Printed in Canada on FSC-certified ancient-forest-free paper (100% post-consumer recycled) that is processed chlorine- and acid-free.

UBC Press is a Benetech Global Certified Accessible™ publisher. The epub version of this book meets stringent accessibility standards, ensuring it is available to people with diverse needs.

Library and Archives Canada Cataloguing in Publication

Title: What could a university be? : revolutionary ideas for the future / Robert Gibbs.

Names: Gibbs, Robert, author

Description: Includes bibliographical references and index.

Identifiers: Canadiana (print) 20250193396 | Canadiana (ebook) 20250193426 | ISBN 9780774839174 (softcover) | ISBN 9780774839181 (PDF) | ISBN 9780774839198 (EPUB)

Subjects: LCSH: College teaching and research. | LCSH: Educational leadership. | LCSH: Educational change. | LCSH: Universities and colleges—Administration. | LCSH: Education, Higher—Forecasting.

Classification: LCC LB2331.3 .G53 2025 | DDC 378.0072—dc23

Canada Council for the Arts | Conseil des arts du Canada

Canada

British Columbia Arts Council

UBC Press gratefully acknowledges the financial support for our publishing program of the Government of Canada, the Canada Council for the Arts, and the British Columbia Arts Council.

UBC Press is situated on the traditional, ancestral, and unceded territory of the xʷməθkʷəy̓əm (Musqueam) people. This land has always been a place of learning for the xʷməθkʷəy̓əm, who have passed on their culture, history, and traditions for millennia, from one generation to the next.

UBC Press
The University of British Columbia
www.ubcpress.ca

For my parents, Richard Gibbs and Jean Gibbs

May their memory be for a blessing

Contents

Preface
A Philosopher Reproved

In December 2010, I was chatting with Natalie Zemon Davis in a café across the street from Honest Ed's, a colourful discount store and beloved Toronto institution. A renowned historian, Natalie had been the director of the Shelby Cullom Davis Center when I was at Princeton. She had been a colleague and mentor for some twenty years.

We were discussing a strategic plan for the Faculty of Arts and Science at the University of Toronto that had just failed dramatically. The plan had been created by a committee at the instruction of the provost, but the dean, Meric Gertler, found himself struggling to defend the committee's proposals, which came down as directives. The proposals included merging several language and literature departments and closing the Centre for Comparative Literature.

Natalie observed that the report was ham-fisted and wouldn't produce the strategic outcomes intended. I said that while some of the proposed changes were plausible, others had ignited such fierce political conflicts inside the university that the dean had clawed them back or sidestepped them. (Despite the controversy, the dean would later become president of the university.)

Just two years before, I'd been appointed as the inaugural director of the Jackman Humanities Institute. My teaching and research had been in various disciplines – philosophy, religion, law, literary studies, and so on – and much of my work was devoted to convening and leading groups of scholars working together in these fields. This experience made me, to my surprise, suitable for this new position. No one enrols as a student, much less completes a PhD, with the hope of becoming a university administrator, but this was an opportunity to engage in hands-on building. The tasks and thinking involved in creating and directing new kinds of humanities research taught me a lot about the challenge of effecting change in the university. The experience also threw into question my assumptions about research.

Humanities centres and institutes began to emerge in the 1960s. Designed to foster new methods and to create thicker interactions among departments, they are typically small research institutes within the humanities sector of a university. Each centre or institute is tailored to its university and culture, and each centre negotiates its limited task with the established humanities departments. There are now about 240 centres worldwide, particularly in the United States, former British Commonwealth countries, and other scattered countries. Every humanities department prizes its intellectual autonomy but struggles with limited resources. At the University of Toronto, the humanities departments long resisted creating a centre, so we joined the game several decades later than most universities.

In 2010, when I spoke with Natalie, the survival of the fledgling Jackman Humanities Institute was not in question, but Natalie reproached me. I should have spoken up to defend the humanities from what looked like an attack by the dean and the strategic plan. In my defence, I pleaded that the new institute depended on balancing the competing demands of the dean, the department chairs, and, of course, humanities professors. I needed, I argued, to keep a low profile and had spoken with the various players privately, trying to play go-between behind the scenes.

Natalie's response was tough (and right). As the most visible administrator in the humanities, I should have spoken up and grabbed attention with the message that the university's humanities departments and professors were wonderful and valuable and creative. I didn't need to attack the dean, but I did need to defend the value of the humanities when the departments were under attack.

Chagrined, I admitted I had missed the train, compromising faculty support for the new institute in the process.

I left the café feeling regretful for what I had not said publicly, grateful for having a friend who felt free to reprove me, and afraid that I would be in a deficit with my fellow humanities scholars for some time (which ended up being true).

But over the next few days, I found myself wondering – why had I failed to rise to the occasion? I had participated in many conversations with the dean, chairs, and leaders and members of the committee, but I had not engaged in the public debate. I had plenty to say, but I was also somehow reticent.

I realized then that I did not know what I thought about the purpose of the university and that I had not studied the history of research universities or even the history of the University of Toronto.

I'm a philosopher, and I was confronting an open question – what is a university for? At the risk of indefinite deferral, I realized I needed to learn about the ideas that informed the history of research universities. Only then could I say something based on thought and knowledge, rather than simply taking sides in an academic battle. I wasn't excused from missing my chance to champion my colleagues in the humanities, but I anticipated that I might find a more creative response to address the conflict.

Like most humanities professors, I think the best way to study something is to teach a course and learn with students. So I put together a first-year undergraduate course on the philosophy of universities over the centuries. I invited Dean Gertler and several other top administrators to come, each for one class. Over time, I delivered multiple versions of the course and delivered talks at various conferences and universities, leading me to the book you're now reading. In one sense, by exploring the ideas in this book, I regained a philosophic voice and role for myself in a context where I was a somewhat unusual academic administrator.

Before that moment in the café with Natalie, my research and teaching focused on a set of mostly twentieth-century Jewish philosophers: Hermann Cohen, Martin Buber, Franz Rosenzweig, Emmanuel Levinas, and Jacques Derrida. I was drawn to them because they had pursued a radical kind of ethics in which my agency arises from responsibility for others. Sometimes responsibility was about being in dialogue, sometimes it was about reading others' words, and sometimes it was expressly about the Bible. In our time, this more radical ethics of responsibility has been a response to the horrors of the Shoah, the murder of European Jews under the Nazis, and the spread of hatred and genocide.

The first step in ethics is listening to the other and realizing I could learn something unexpected and be called to respond. This ethical lens also led me to focus on social institutions, particularly law and courts. A court, a school, a hospital, or even a legislature can become a site where we can discern responsibilities supported or betrayed. In personal face-to-face relations, we are responsible for the people close to us; institutions should protect the other person and can even foster our ability to take care of one another. Ethical ideas in these institutions are not checklists or ethics protocols but rather a kind of thinking and searching – a discernment of how our social goals can be furthered in institutions.

Following the end of my term as director of the Jackman Humanities Institute, I spoke at universities and drafted chapters for a book on the responsibility of the university. I was honoured to be invited to be the J.V. Clyne Lecturer at the University of British Columbia's Green College from January to April 2019. It was during this period that this book came into focus in conversation with UBC Press.

And then the world at large and the universities in particular entered an unprecedented time of storm and challenge. The COVID-19 pandemic, Black Lives Matter, the January 6 insurrection in the United States, the launch of ChatGPT, the wars in Ukraine and Gaza, to say nothing of the intellectual threats of misinformation campaigns – it has been a rough time, with the challenges to universities getting ever sharper. To launch this book at this time is a specific dare – how can what I had sketched as a creative future for universities still promise to frame a university looking forward from our moment of crisis?

What I discovered is that in the face of these and other problems, such as the battle over that strategic plan, universities often become stuck in conflicts arising from their leaders' tutelage to underexamined ideas. A philosophical exploration of ideas about the university can help loosen up and reframe problems; it can offer new ways to articulate the university's goals. In short, by reflecting philosophically and historically on ideas about the university, we can empower those seeking to reimagine the university of the future.

To do this, I examine a set of ideas – knowledge, critique, unity, freedom, and replication – that traditionally informed understandings of what universities are for and often come to mind in attempts to articulate what a university does. Unsurprisingly, they are often at play in conversations, vision statements, and political arguments and lie at the core of how administrators and professors understand the university.

But I also discuss a second set of ideas – inquiry, discord, multiplication, study, permeability, and responsibility. These ideas are often missing in discussions of the university's purpose. These ideas shift the focus to students and their education. They hold the answers to the key question: how can we transform our universities so that higher education continues to be the most potent vehicle for solving the many challenges of our demanding times?

In many ways, this book is a humanities-based response to that strategic plan and its pitched battles. My position directing a humanities research institute required a bold public defence of the humanities, and my philosophical and historical expertise has since allowed me to study and contemplate better models for the research university. I hope these ideas will help us formulate better justifications for the university and a university education. The ideas that follow arose out of humanities research. This book is not a public policy proposal or an apology for liberal arts education and humanities departments. I believe these sets of ideas can help us bring into focus the goal of research to transform universities for the future.

WHAT COULD
A UNIVERSITY BE?

Introduction
What Is University Education For?

We live in a time of massive problems, from climate change to systemic racism, from the challenges of immigration to injustice, from pandemics to the flood of information. We need new solutions, new insights, new policies, new technology, but we have little time. The future is leaning hard on today. The university is a venerable institution, but if it can't help us now, then it has no future.

Many voices in society today are calling on the university to discover new knowledge, to connect with social movements, to incubate new technologies, to innovate on social policy, to explore history to grasp what needs to change now. Universities are hearing these calls, and when they're backed by funding, they often rush to help. But being venerable just as often leads to hesitation and even resistance to these calls. On campus, we're suspicious of the hands that feed us – government, corporations, professional associations, big pharma, IT ... Can the university interact with society and help?

Many professors and administrators are responding to these calls. We have new programs, initiatives, pilot projects, strategic plans, and so on. Recent PhDs, new professors, established professors, and deans and provosts are feeling the push and pull to transform research universities. Elite universities are paying more attention to student research. Others have launched programs to engage society beyond the university through co-ops, programs in serviced learning, and research exchanges. Funders are focusing on research partnerships. Vice-presidents are linking research to innovation and knowledge transfer. Library programs are fostering digital media literacy. Laboratories are being built for inquiry- and team-based learning. Urban universities are partnering up with their cities and approaching research in new ways. Public universities are reimagining their local responsibilities.

For each of these efforts, there are people beyond the university who are meeting and even calling for even bolder change. The research university is a place where people are learning how to think beyond the present and the past, to cultivate future possibilities.

But when we try to rethink the research university's goal, to move beyond the current moment, the future of the research university is uncertain and confused. This confusion stems from trying to do too many things. But it's also a side effect of what Christopher Newfield, a professor of literature and American studies and recently a director of research, calls the "great mistake": the importation of business management as a task for university leaders and governors.[1]

I would hazard that the greatest obstacle to thinking deeply and seriously about universities is a specific model of management that governs the lives of administrators and leads to a scarcity of time to think about universities, especially about the ideas of universities.

To read this book, deans, chairs, provosts, and presidents would have to make real interruptions in their schedules. The job of running our universities has changed in such a way that the people who most need to reflect and imagine the shape of higher education are prevented and distracted by the myriad tasks of administration and management. And risk management dictates clichéd and minimal explanation of higher education's goals. Who, then, is left to do this thinking?

I offer a simplified model. I distinguish three different roles in terms of their domains of responsibility: people who lead the university have responsibility for (1) things, (2) other people, and (3) ideas.

I'm not a professor of management, but let me suggest that "administration" is the responsibility for things, including buildings, food, schedules, and information infrastructure. It is the administrator's duty to arrange and provide the things needed in an enterprise.

Let me then call "management" responsibility for other people. People are harder to cope with than things – people push back, so management depends on authority in complex ways. The university is a difficult place to manage people because professors are not simply employees in a business (nor are graduate students). Governance is ideally collegial, and authority is much more attenuated. But many of our administrators are preoccupied with control and responsibility for things *and* people.

Let me then propose that responsibility for ideas is "leadership." Leadership is the vision or guidance that allows things and people to align and work for an idea. Leadership typically also requires people and things because ideas set goals for institutions. In this sense, a leader is not simply an officeholder (any more than being a manager makes one skilled at coordinating and managing people). Rather, a leader is someone who can frame and explore ideas in a way that allows other people and things to work together.

Because our current moment requires better university leadership, revising the ideas that set forth the task for our universities is vital.

Many of the people making the most creative changes in research universities are not in traditional roles – they are not presidents, provosts, deans, chairs, or leading research professors. Instead, some belong to an expanding cohort of people in what is called the teaching stream. Some are teaching multiple undergraduate courses; others are running undergraduate teaching laboratories; others are directing new interdisciplinary programs. Many others occupy new positions in the offices of deans and provosts.

Often, they are people designing and implementing initiatives that focus on undergraduates and other students. They are designing new paths toward community engagement. They are the people making the university's research mission connect more with society.

When I set out to write this book, I had two groups of readers in mind – traditional leaders and this new brand of professor and administrator. I hoped the ideas I explored in this book would help them better articulate the goals to which many of them were already committed. But today I realize there are people inside the university (especially students) and outside who are rethinking, perhaps even questioning, the purpose of research and higher education.

There are many university prophets in our time, scholars who are speaking and writing about the future and addressing the questions of concern here. How can universities improve our world? Some have rousingly defended universities as places where discovery and invention can help transform a world that is unknown and uncertain. Some have championed a more entrepreneurial image of universities as places, like a business, committed to innovation. Some have extolled the university's fostering of critical thinking and linked it to an increase in democracy.

Out of these debates, a new field has emerged – critical university studies. One of its leaders, Christopher Newfield, recognizes that funding models in the United States have shifted from the public sphere and its shared vision to private funders with local, often profit-driven goals. Conflicting viewpoints among scholars can help us identify general ideas about the university's future, but many of these scholars are located in the US context, within a system that has many unusual characteristics.

Here, the Canadian research university is the model. Although it's a bit of an exaggeration to say that there's a Canadian "system" for universities (education is a provincial matter in Canada), the promise and goals of research universities throughout Canada are largely congruent. Moreover, many of these goals are shared around the world, including in Australia, China, and Europe where there's no hierarchy of small elite universities or colleges such as Harvard or Yale above the major comprehensive research universities. As in Canada, the best universities are large, urban, and public.

My goal is to reimagine the research university by building on the system we already have. The set of new ideas proposed here can be distributed more widely, including in US universities classified as "R:1 Doctoral Universities" and even in private elite universities.

Directing a Humanities Institute

Over the years, I've learned several maxims. One is that no administrative job is what you expect it will be. When I was first appointed to direct the Humanities Centre at the University of Toronto, I had little sense of how research was done outside of my fields or how it was funded. Indeed, I had no idea that a generous and truly magnificent donor was ready to engage in conversations about a major gift that would lead to the founding of the Jackman Humanities Institute. Hal and Maruja

Jackman's gift, when augmented by the university's commitments, came to $90.3 million. In short, the job I signed up for was vastly more interesting and exciting than I thought it would be.

We sought advice from leaders in the humanities and saw that one of the key challenges of an urban university is its size. The humanities departments at the University of Toronto are large. Even now, English and History have about ninety professors each and Philosophy has sixty. And there are almost 750 PhD students in the humanities. We addressed the size issue by focusing on activities that would draw people together who would not normally interact: professors from different departments, different campuses and, more radically, different faculties. To sidestep resistance to what many felt was a diversion of resources from their departments, we designed the Jackman Humanities Institute to not compete with the departments. The institute had no permanent professors, no courses, no degree programs. Instead, we built a research-only institute with a strong sense of circulation, where no single group or school could claim the institute for its own.

The director reports to a council of humanities institute deans, and soon after we began, our roster expanded to ten faculties, including Law, Education, Music, Information, Architecture and Design, and the library. We felt the ongoing tension between the humanities and other faculties, but it was a healthy, if tricky, tension because it led the other faculties to think more about their relations with the humanities and the broader role and goals of the humanities in the university.

My role as director of the institute came with many university committee appointments: Academic Board, the Library Committee, and the Research Advisory Board, to name a few. In these roles, I learned that humanities research was not often understood or recognized, and I realized I needed to learn how research worked in other contexts. The health sciences, for instance, had come into being in tandem with a series of hospitals and much of the research was in an area called fundamental science, not directly linked to clinical education. Other professional faculties were engaged in entrepreneurial innovation as the outcome of their research.

In short, the world of university research is not flat. Most professors know only about the shape and purpose of research in their own fields, a limitation that contributes to misunderstandings about the nature and purpose of research.

In the first years, the institute adopted programs of two sizes: small annual residential circles of fellows of under twenty people, and large working groups and a Program for the Arts that reached across the university to engage participants through lectures, workshops, and exhibitions. We funded ten to twelve working groups a year, each with fifteen to twenty professors and graduate students. The Program for the Arts supported about fifteen events a year. Although these events were a small portion of the public events held at the University of Toronto each year, they were held across the campuses and disciplines and collectively drew thousands of attendees – helping to give the humanities a more public face.

Because the founding donation and the university's matching funds were staged, we established our basic programs and tried a dozen other short-term experiments before the second phase of programming began. To design this second phase, we convened a new series of workshops with international leaders, many of whom also had significant resources, and we sought their advice. Perhaps the most important advice we got was from Tracey McIntosh, professor of Indigenous studies at the University of Auckland and director of New Zealand's Māori Centre of Research Excellence, Ngā Pae o te Māramatanga.

McIntosh offered this insight from her own centre: to take the next step, we needed to create a way for scholars to contribute their own energy and expertise to the institute's programs. We established new research communities. Each had a three-to-five-year life cycle; each had a director who would lead a project in their area of expertise with the support of a recent PhD administrator; and each would include a wide range of participants, professors, and graduate students from different faculties and generations and people from outside our university. We hoped to bring together professors already engaged in these kinds of research, support them for a limited time, and then release the communities to find homes in or outside the university.

This phase was a kind of nursery that put three different projects into motion during my time: (1) a one-month summer residential research program for humanities undergraduates working with professors, (2) a digital humanities network that brought together two hundred or so graduate students and professors developing new modes of research with information technology, and (3) a south-north dialogue between the University of Toronto and the University of the Western Cape in South Africa, each exploring similar topics in very different cultural and university contexts.

These communities seeded the argument of this book. Directing the research institute placed me outside the hierarchy and structures of deans and department chairs. I was absorbed in the task of exploring and fostering humanities research, often quite far from my philosophical world. I was able to see obliquely what is often experienced only vertically. That is, most professors and administrators, to say nothing of students, experience the university either from the top down (the dominant experience) or the bottom up. But I saw how the institution regulated research and education in service to various forces and how program changes and new practices were regularly blocked from going up or down.

One chair warned that because I was working outside the hierarchy, the work could be dangerous for me. I replied that the Jackman Humanities Institute was endowed to work outside the hierarchy and was not at risk. Nevertheless, the chair clearly thought my own standing could be easily compromised. Of course, the risks wouldn't endanger my secured professorial position, but they might subvert any hopes I had to support research that did not reside easily within the departments. I had the exceptional privilege of experimenting while insulated from the normal tensions and forces within the university, and this position landed me in an unfamiliar space where people debated which changes were desirable and how to make them happen.

This unusual vantage point combined with my philosophical background eventually led me to ponder a bold set of questions about the research university and the future. Beyond the future that is the prophet's province, there's a deeper future that animates the research university, one that emerges from a more philosophical angle. Prophets foretell the future: they tell us what will happen. Much of science aims to know and control the future. By applying laws and probabilities, it determines what will certainly happen. But education is also about learning how to create new possibilities, about the rigorous thinking that can hold the future open for change and previously unknown laws and events.

The time of research is a future that does not yet exist. It is not, necessarily, an extension of the present. When we explore the idea of research, we see that an open future is one where our universities can help us make new knowledge, new policies, new medicines, and new ways of grasping the truths about our past. We can, indeed, revise our sense of what the research university is for by rethinking the future, as such.[2]

The goals of a liberal education might not fit or be countable in the metrics for research universities. The value of its ideas might not count or appear within the metrics of university funding or entrepreneurialism. And yet the search for ideas and the assertion of their value is shared by many prophets of the university.

I do not use the term *ideas* idly or colloquially. I do not use it haphazardly, as John Henry Newman does in his iconic *The Idea of a University,* where the word is never defined, rarely used, and seems to have no more than a general sense of view or notion.[3] In this book, an idea is something that exceeds our experience and gives it direction. Like a goal, a vision, or a norm, an idea guides the work of an institution and its organized series of practices.

Philosophers disagree about what ideas are and what they do in our thinking. Ideas, in my interpretation, are not eternal. As we'll explore, any idea of the university is deeply historical, but I choose ideas for the future. I hope to contribute to these debates at the philosophical level of ideas because I believe ideas can open up and direct new ways of thinking about higher education.

Here, I examine philosophical and historical accounts of universities and reflect on some possibilities that were carefully described but never pursued. This history of what didn't happen helps us see that the universities of today are contingent – their past and present could have been otherwise. Universities have gone through many phases: church-mandated censorship, colonial exclusion of Indigenous knowledge, and the neoliberal "great mistake"; none of these developments were fated.

Perhaps this is the great contribution of the humanities – to unmoor our ship, stuck in the present and bound to break up on the rocks. My research and the thinking that pervades these pages examine what could have been and what might yet be. It makes clear some real possibilities for how we can refashion our universities to enhance our collective future.

This book takes a curious path. It invites you into each chapter with a question prominent in today's debates and then leads to deeper conflicts where rich insight can be found. There is a pattern of inquiry. You have already seen it in action in the preface, where I describe being reproached for not standing up for the humanities, which led to me questioning why I didn't, which led to an open question – What are research universities for?

Often the first questions asked call us to take a stand, to line up on one side of a political debate or the other. Yes, the humanities are important, and their professors are doing groundbreaking, valuable work. However, pausing to reflect on what humanities research is, who it's for, and how teaching and research are linked in our research universities opens more questions, questions that can't be resolved by a who-is-not-with-us-is-against-us logic. These first questions often fall into what philosophy calls the law of excluded middle.

Each chapter will lead you not to an answer but to deeper questions, and those questions are in the service of supporting changes already emerging within our universities and yet to come. Drawing lines and choosing sides won't get us ahead in the search for a better education for our students. Indeed, this book illuminates where those oppositions first emerged and at times deconstructs them. A clear blueprint for change is not on offer. Instead, I offer a valuable rethinking of what higher education is for and the kinds of thinking we want our students to learn.

Upside Down, Round and Round, and Inside Out

First of all, whose research counts at universities? In the metrics for research universities, the professors' research dominates. But I propose that students are the key to understanding the research university's goals.

Chapter 1 revisits the debates surrounding the founding of the research university in early nineteenth-century Germany to help refine the idea of inquiry as the focus of education in research universities. There are other modes of higher education: education in trades and technical skills, education in established knowledge systems and traditions, and education focused on critical thinking and learning how to learn. The latter two are often advanced for the university in relation to the idea of knowledge and the idea of critique. But I propose we can educate tens of thousands of undergraduates to inquire and discover new knowledge. Philosophical reflection provides a heightened sense of the future for students at research universities – training in thinking that will not limit them to learning knowledge that emerges elsewhere but teaches them to become creators of new knowledge.

In Chapter 2, I risk disrupting many models of the research university by arguing that we should turn it upside down – that the flow of inquiry should come from undergraduates. Often, PhD students are the focus of discussions about teaching research, because they are taken to represent where teaching and research meet. But the collapse of a market for new professors within the university casts PhD programs into a dubious role.

Chapter 2 offers the idea of multiplication in lieu of the idea of replication. The goal is to dramatically expand beyond the university the number of people engaged in research, the number of people creating the knowledge and insight we need for the future. In the upside-down research university, PhD students learn how to conduct research by teaching undergraduate students how to do research, that is, how to inquire and explore. The professor is not an autocrat who presides over a research team, the only one who can truly create new knowledge. Instead, the professor is the one who teaches others how to teach and how to inquire into new knowledge. The idea of multiplication meets the needs of society today – a society of questions more than a knowledge economy – because it educates people to explore and innovate, to inquire and to create the future on a much greater scale.

Chapter 3 tackles a profound problem – the disruptions of information technologies – by drawing on an unusual resource. New communication technologies not only bypass the authority of the university and its experts – they threaten the truth of science and the Socratic liberal values required for education. Artificial intelligence is poised to displace many university-trained professions and maybe professors too. How will students who are born digital engage with this new world? And what place does higher education hold in a world of widely distributed (and distorted) information?

I suggest that the skills of collecting, commenting, and editing – the bedrock of humanities scholarship – are distinctly valuable to the new world of social media and that the university (and the humanities, especially) can educate students to develop the skills and reasoning necessary to contribute and innovate in the new reading and writing of our time.

The humanities' ability to explore history shows us how the past (and thus the future) is not fated. I look back to the fifteenth and sixteenth centuries, when the new technology of printing changed the regime of study and the control of information. The idea of unity of all knowledge is no longer adequate for guiding universities. Despite the novel challenges of our time, looking back to the way that reading changed in that era helps frame an idea of discord, which can be used to negotiate with plural and conflicting ways of justifying knowledge. The task here is to figure out how to reach across these divides and resist using terror to silence other kinds of knowledge.

In Chapter 4, I explore how the many schools in a university can help sustain diverse relations within society. Medieval universities emerged to provide training for the professions (law, medicine, and religion), and large faculties in urban universities are still professional schools. These schools are intimately connected to society and its needs and are often regulated by professional bodies that set the standards for the accreditation of the university's degrees. These students are learning how to think like a doctor, teacher, lawyer, engineer ... and the logic of inquiry. The university comprises the whole gamut of students and professors. Between the schools, there's conflict and disagreement about what counts as research and what a student needs to learn. But these conflicts reveal that in discord there's a creative possibility.

This plurality in the university helps foster the second transformation, which goes round and round (literally a revolution). The capacity to create new insight and help address the problems of the world can be enhanced by discord and different perspectives on what knowledge is – if we embrace discord as a positive element of the university.

To accentuate the tension between the idea of responsibility and the idea of freedom, I examine the question: Where do research questions come from? Research is a response to questions, and its results emerge with a certain kind of freedom.

In Chapter 5, I argue that we should also turn the university inside out – that the flow of research questions should come from society rather than from within. To accomplish this, universities will need to exchange knowledge and expertise with diverse groups in society. Indeed, the calls from society – from business, government, the information technology sector, arts institutions, political activists, religious communities, and others – suggest future partnerships and the promise of change. Each call is a request for new insight and a requisition for graduating students as the embodied future, the greatest promise. University students can learn how to navigate and embody the exchange of knowledge and questions in research. In our large urban universities, they are already in motion, living in the city and studying at the university. I call this an urban epistemology. The idea of permeability will guide us to see how students' commuting between the two places and living with the tension between society and the university can advance the goal of teaching students the logic of inquiry.

I hope you won't be surprised to read that these three bold proposals – turning the university upside down, round and round, and inside out – have met with much resistance in our research universities. Our status in comparison with other universities, our funding from private and public sources, and our intellectual formation are all currently seen as being dependent on professors and their research accomplishments.

Through the recourse to new ideas, we can lead a change in research universities. The line of argument then contrasts newer ideas with older ones, and this table summarizes the arguments of the chapters.

	What a University Is	*What a University Could Be*
Introduction		Idea of Study
Chapter 1	Idea of Knowledge Idea of Critique	Idea of Inquiry
Chapter 2	Idea of Replication	Idea of Multiplication
Chapter 3	Idea of Unity	Idea of Discord
Chapter 4	Idea of Freedom	Idea of Responsibility
Chapter 5		Idea of Permeability

We don't need to invent new practices and projects, as many initiatives are already underway. But because each step forward often meets with practical – and principled – resistance, we need a better case to support these changes. We need a better account of the promise of research – to persuade administrators and funders to provide resources, to enable professors to see how they can play a contributing role in teaching the logic of inquiry, and to connect with students' creative capacities.

We need a better justification for our research universities, a more honest account of what we can contribute. Students, particularly undergraduates, are the future of research. Let us teach them the logic of inquiry: how to research, how to inquire into what is unknown. The research university should educate them to create knowledge that is lacking. With them as our focus, let us remodel how questions and research flow between society and the university. They hold out the promise of learning how to create new knowledge, of creating new solutions for our failing world.

Students and Study

If the goal of this book is to lead us to think about the future in a philosophical way that goes beyond debates about economics and democracy, it must also circle back from this reflection. We need to think more concretely about the people in the university, particularly the largest group of people who have the richest meaning of the future: students. If research is about creating new insights and new questions and new knowledge, the people who should be learning how to do this at a research university are the students: the undergraduates, the PhDs, the professional students – all the students should be learning the logic of inquiry: they are the future.

As obvious as this may seem, it typically goes unsaid: to be a student is ... to study. Students are not clients; they are not consumers; they are not users who can be "captured" by outcomes, indicators, or throughputs. Experts recognize this fact, yet study is not a main theme or even a topic in the shelf of books I have on recent debates. Few philosophical arguments about the future of the university analyze what it means to study.

So before we go any further, let the first idea of this book be the idea of study. What, this humanities professor asks, does the word *student* mean? In the academic field of higher education, students are the subject matter for vast research. But philosophers often examine what seems obvious, and, to me, this idea of study especially has the power to help reorient the research university.

Framing the idea of study means making explicit a goal that exceeds our current practices. Framing the idea of study does not mean offering an empirical account of what students today "do." Rather, it is an attempt to identify the ideas that may guide them. With some irony, I'll try to outline the idea of study by exploring the words *student* and *study* as documented by the *Oxford English Dictionary*, which emerged from the philological research of great humanities scholars.

So let me link, or turn to, the 1989 version of the *Oxford English Dictionary*, conveniently available to students and faculty online.

> *student, n.*
> 1. A person who is engaged in or addicted to study.
> 2. a. A person who is undergoing a course of study and instruction at a university or other place of higher education or technical training. Also const. *of*, *in* (a subject); often with defining word prefixed, as *art student, law student, medical student.*

The *Oxford English Dictionary* traces the use of the word in the first sense back to 1398 and in the second sense to 1450.

Notice first that the second definition focuses on "a course of study" and presumes that this is higher education (or what some might call postsecondary training). Students are, in this case, the people who are at a university to get something called "higher education." Labelling primary and secondary pupils "students" is of more recent usage (and from the United States). So historically speaking, it's not amiss to confine our thinking here to university students. We also have three professional students as examples – art, law, and medical students – indicating that the term *student* links to the professions not haphazardly.

Of course, the more interesting definition is the first one, which speaks to the person and, indeed, to an affect. If the second definition addresses the institution and the purpose, then the first definition speaks of the personal quality of being engaged in or addicted to study. A student is not a passive recipient or vehicle for knowledge. A student is not a consumer of skills or know-how but directly engaged, and *engaged*, of course, could mean, according to the dictionary, anything from "being entangled with" to "committing or being in bond to." But the word that leaps out from the first definition is *addicted*. A student has a study habit she cannot shake. She needs to study, wants to study, cannot stop (and doesn't want to). A student is bound up with study and studies not from calculation but because of an almost overpowering bond or commitment.

This may seem extreme. But let's move on to the next keyword – *study*.

> *study, n.*
> 1. In certain senses of Latin *studium* (chiefly in translations from Latin): Affection, friendliness, devotion to another's welfare; partisan sympathy; desire, inclination; pleasure or interest felt in something. *Obs.*
> 2. ...
> 3. a. A state of mental perplexity or anxious thought. Sometimes with indirect question: Doubt whether, etc. *Obs.*
> ...
> 5. a. Application of mind to the acquisition of learning; mental labour, reading and reflection directed to learning, literary composition, invention, or the like.

The last definition is the most recognizable. But definition 3a, an obsolete one (last used in the late seventeenth century), captures the quality, as it were, of learning. It focuses on anxiety and perplexity. To be addicted to study is to be caught in perplexity, to be living in the questions; it is to be more keenly aware that the future is uncertain and, hence, to study is to provoke anxiety. Obsolete (or not), this definition of *study* is very much a part of the lives of students today.

As for the first meaning, well, that takes us beyond the grasp of knowing into the world of desires and enthusiasm: "Affection, friendliness, devotion to another's welfare; partisan sympathy; desire, inclination;

pleasure or interest felt in something." This is not a disinterested mind but one alive with care and pleasure and concern for others' needs, with, I would suggest, others' questions.

The first definition goes on to captures the word's etymology in a delightfully scholarly (or studied) way along a trusty route from the Latin *studium* to the English *study*.

> [Old French] *estudie* masc. (later *estuide*, *estude* masc. and fem., [modern French] *étude* fem.) = [Provençal] *estudi-s*, *estuzi-s*, [Spanish] *estúdio*, [Portuguese] *estudo*, [Italian] *studio*, ad. Latin *studium*, zeal, affection, painstaking, study, related to *studēre* to be zealous, seek to be helpful, apply oneself, study.

The Latin word expresses care, energy, and affection but also zeal. These meanings were transferred from Latin as the word spread into the vernacular languages of Europe. We have a root for the university in this desire and zeal, this engagement with learning.

We can frame the idea of study from this history of the words *student* and *study*. The idea encapsulates an image of passion in university education that is linked to the professions and rigorous thought. As we explore what students should learn in university within the claim that universities should exist primarily for students, we need to hold in mind the eagerness, the desire, yes, even the addiction, that brings them to the university. There are other paths to power, prestige, money, and information. For many, becoming a university student may not be a choice but rather something expected of them. But the experience of studying reaches its highest level when it's fuelled by the desire, even the addiction, mentioned in these dictionary entries.

> **THE IDEA OF STUDY.** The application of the mind to the acquisition of learning; mental labour, reading, and reflection directed to learning, literary composition, and invention. A devotion of time and effort to the pursuit of knowledge; a passionate desire to learn in the university often linked to the professions. Students are those committed to studying.

As with the other ideas, every student will subscribe to the idea of study to various degrees. An idea of something allows us to see the best or deepest goal of the activity. To focus on students is to focus, then, on the highest possibility of the university as a home to this sort of study. At the centre of ideas for the university is the idea of study.

1

Teaching Undergraduates to Do Research

On a beautiful May afternoon in 2017, the Scholars in Residence program, sponsored by the Jackman Humanities Institute, held a research colloquium after a month spent conducting research in groups made up of one humanities professor and five undergraduates. The students and professors presented reports that demonstrated the success of the program. One group, led by Eva-Lynn Jagoe, had proposed to focus on social movements and activism, but their research morphed into an examination of students' experiences as recent immigrants or children of immigrants. Their report at the colloquium took the form of students telling one another's stories of immigration and crossing ethnic boundaries, religious divisions, and genders. It was clear to everyone that a month spent investigating their diverse experiences in Canada had produced a strong sense of a research community, significant insights into the challenges of immigration, and the power of telling stories.

After the presentations, I spoke with Eva-Lynn, who was enthusiastic. She said working with these students had been one of the best teaching experiences she'd had at our university. The students surprised her because she'd learned so much from them. But when I asked her whether this sort of research experience could be expanded widely to our undergraduates, she demurred. These students, she said, were the *crème de la crème*. Indeed. For the ten projects we ran that year, we'd selected fifty students from almost one thousand applicants. All of them had a minimum

GPA of 3.0. We started with the top students and from there skimmed the top 5 percent.

As I enjoyed a festive dinner with the students, I was struck by just how impressive and impassioned they were. I told them so (a sentiment echoed by other professors in the group too) and related that they were the crème de la crème. But I also asked them if they thought other undergraduates could benefit from serious humanities research opportunities. Perhaps they were modest about their own brilliance, but each person at the table said yes and mentioned friends, roommates, and others. They thought there were many (maybe a thousand or more, I thought) who would enjoy and benefit from learning how to do research.

But they had one caveat: professors would need to do a better job of explaining to students what research was. The students thought they had been lucky in applying and being selected, but few of them, and even fewer of their friends, understood what humanities research was.

It is curious that the key index of status for universities is the research conducted by their professors and yet the vast majority of participants in university life are its undergraduates. While professors aspire to tenured (permanent) positions and seem to be the university, students flow through the university. If we recognize that the goal of the institution should address this flow, then we need to ask two questions. Why do so many undergraduate students come to our universities? And what are they learning?

There are several familiar answers to these questions. Students want to get a job or to become job-ready. International students often want to see another part of the world. For some students, the social context is the draw. But what role does education itself play? For some, students are getting something called formation or access to traditions of learning; for others, students are learning critical thinking skills (learning to learn how to learn); for still others, students are getting a chance to participate in research.

The thousand applicants we received that summer, and the steady stream of applicants we experienced in the years that followed, showed us that students are more eager to learn how to do research than professors think they are.

Thinking about university only in terms of job preparation hides a key question. What do students need to learn to qualify for their future jobs?

Research requires learning a kind of thinking that I call the logic of inquiry. Critical thinking examines how knowledge is created and proven. Formation is a kind of thinking that focuses on acquiring knowledge and moral insights. Vocational training is learning a body of knowledge and a set of practices and skills in a trade. Each of these four kinds of learning might qualify one for a job, and each addresses the needs of society beyond the university.

The logic of inquiry, critical thinking, formation, and vocational training often overlap. Professors often love to focus on their research, but they can also love teaching undergraduates. They devote care and time and creative thinking to communicating with their students. But how can they combine their research (often referred to as "my work") with their undergraduate teaching?

Here, we face a classic polarity, with scholarship and the advancement of science at one pole and the education of students at the other. The research universities we know are hugely committed to research for the advancement of knowledge, which is now linked explicitly to research's economic and social impact. Measured by money spent, universities are the site of almost half the research in society, but this pursuit of new science is not well understood in the wider world. (There is one exception, medicine, which almost everyone valued until the COVID-19 pandemic.) Despite reductions in corporate research and development budgets, a lot of research still happens in industrial settings. When a new drug, a new app, or an improvement to energy production is discovered, the research is vindicated by the invention and the profits generated.

But what about research in fields such as subatomic physics, etymology, quantum computing, ethnomusicology or, dare I add, philosophy? Few would dispute that discovering new things is good, but aside from our human desire to know, how do we justify research that may seem arcane, basic, pure, creative, or artistic?

After the Second World War, the research side of the university expanded with state funding that came in response to arguments that the accumulation of information and new knowledge would combine to produce real benefits to society: social science research would improve society, natural science research would create better weapons for warfare (to say nothing of our technology-based economies), medical research would extend life and fight disease, the study of languages would contribute to the Cold War. These days, universities are gobbling up national science laboratories, making universities the leading location for research and attracting corporate partnerships.

Research often seems to be the central function of the universities – the source of their status and their main contribution to society. The professors' research and their teams are the focus, with only an occasional nod to the university's role in educating highly qualified personnel (that is, a small cadre of research assistants) and its PhD programs, which exist to produce (or replicate) professors. Because professors are selected, trained, and rewarded for cutting-edge research, they fear anything that might divert attention away from or alter the validity of their findings or the authority of their practices.

I propose we change the index of excellence from the amount of money brought into the university via a professor's research to the number of students involved in learning how to do research. Excellence for a research university would thus be measured by how well it taught its students the logic of inquiry – how to do research.

In the current system, state research boards and corporate funding tend to support this focus on research. But in the Canadian system, state support revolves around students and the public's belief that education matters. Which brings us to the other pole and question. What should students in research universities be learning?

When forming the Jackman Humanities Institute, I travelled and canvassed many humanities centres and institutes to learn how they worked. A common feature was an annual circle of fellows composed primarily of professors bought out of some or all of their teaching responsibilities to pursue their research. We adopted this practice and opted for a themed circle each year: "telling stories", "food," "location/dislocation," "image and spectacle," "translation and the multiplicity of languages," "time, rhythm, and pace," and so on. Each week, we held a seminar. After a catered lunch, one of the fellows presented their work, and the others asked questions and discussed the material.

The dean of the Faculty of Arts and Science (a physicist) and the university's president (a public health doctor) strongly encouraged us to include undergraduates in our programs. But when I visited the other centres, I noticed that if they had undergraduate fellows, they didn't participate in the lunch seminars. I asked the director of the prestigious Stanford University Humanities Center if they ever included undergraduates. He said they'd tried for a few years, but the undergraduates felt unable and unready to contribute to the discussions. The students then got their own table in an adjoining room. The kids' table, I thought.

Intergenerational learning is a characteristic of universities in general. When we included four stages of fellows at the Jackman Humanities Institute (professors, postdoctoral fellows, PhD students, and undergraduate students) and encouraged them to learn and work with one another in a research environment, new energy and insights emerged. Each undergraduate was supervised by a professor, and often this was not a proper disciplinary fit. Moreover, unlike the PhD students and the postdocs, the undergraduates had not yet been fully disciplined, so their passion and curiosity were greater. They had not been trained to ignore extradisciplinary issues and methods, so they were less constrained.

In short, the undergraduates showed the greatest insight and creativity in research. At the end of the first year, one student commented that she'd had a real education. At first, she said, she'd been intimidated and felt unready to comment on the other fellows' presentations. She could only listen. But the mixed-generation seminar environment showed her how to engage in the discussion and raise a question based on her own perspective and research. Later, in the winter, she learned how to make what she considered (and I agreed) were the best kind of comments – comments or questions that would help the presenter develop their work. In the space of one year, she'd gone from engaging in a kind of listening, to absorbing information, to a mode of critical questioning, to genuinely collaborative inquiry.

For me, the discovery that inquiry could flow from the undergraduates to the rest of the circle (complementing the more expected flow from professors to postdocs to graduate students) made me contemplate other ways a research university might amplify a student's desire to create new knowledge.

We had six undergraduate fellows a year, but from the outset, I thought the institute could lead explorations in undergraduates learning the logic of inquiry. But there was resistance. Given the size of our university and its research focus, undergraduates were not recognized as a focus for research education. In other words, as the student at the dinner for Scholars in Residence had said, professors had not made the nature of humanities research clear to students.

That Scholars in Residence dinner had emerged from an experiment in our second phase. A colleague suggested we look at a project at Harvard, the Cultural Agents Initiative, in which students engaged in arts research in the community in the summer. We adapted, piloted, and expanded the program to suit our university. Undergraduates lived in our college residences for one month and worked in teams of five on an aspect of a professor's research. In 2016, in a rushed proof of concept, we had four professors and twenty students. In our second year, we had ten professors and fifty students. The professors were from six different schools and had remarkably diverse projects. After the ringing success of that year, including Eva-Lynn Jagoe's students' explorations of the challenges of immigration and powerful storytelling, the Jackman Humanities Institute drew matching support from the colleges, the provost, and the vice-president of research and innovation. Of course, a project for 50 students (now scaled up to 150) is only a drop in the bucket. But creating a creative, nurturing cohort of professors who wanted to work with undergraduates on research was the kind of task the Jackman Humanities Institute had set out to accomplish.

The model of undergraduates doing research with professors in the summer is familiar – even dominant – in the natural sciences and has been so for decades. But the humanities are more conservative, and their professors normally prefer solitary research. So it was interesting to see the huge uptake from students eager to participate in research. Even though humanities research is far from being an entrepreneurial activity, it offers students the kind of learning they value and that they expect others in society to desire too.

Across the university, the presumption is that only the very best undergraduate students (students who are preparing to undertake a PhD, students who professors hope will one day succeed them as professors) are candidates to learn the logic of inquiry. This presumption reflects the university's hierarchy and the gap between research and undergraduate teaching. Provoked by these experiments and similar experiments at other institutions, I propose that we reexamine this presumption to form a different view of the relationship between research and undergraduate education. Although this is an old debate, I propose that we can distinguish the idea of inquiry from the idea of knowledge and the idea of critique.

The idea of inquiry is the thinking that defines research itself. The claim is simple and bold: at a research university, every student at every stage should be learning how to do research. The promise of undergraduate students is the hope that they will learn how to discover new insights, invent new techniques, and create new laws and new ways to make our society more just. I hold that this view of higher education will offer the greatest benefit to society: a huge number of people from every community and class who have learned how to inquire.

Historical Models: Three Ideas

My interest in determining how research universities can best help society is bound to our current moment and our past. The past is not a string of inevitable developments. On the contrary, to look back is to see paths not taken. My mode of inquiry, common in the humanities, is to explore historical possibilities that did not come to pass to critique the current moment and imagine future possibilities for the university.

Resistance to educating all students in the logic of inquiry stems, in part, from ideas that don't match up with these new hopes. To find an answer to the question, What kind of thinking should students be learning?, let's go back to the birth of the research university. Berlin, 1810.

Not long after its founding, the University of Berlin became the paradigm of the research university. This is a point of pride because the university was founded before Germany was a unified state. Calls came for the Prussian state and its capital, Berlin, to take the lead because, it was felt, a new university would be especially important for creating an educated class to run Germany's emerging state apparatus.

While we in Canada and elsewhere would not expect philosophy professors to dominate a public debate, several philosophers wrote proposals and debated the founding of this new university. Philosophical ideas circulated widely. F.W.J. Schelling wrote an essay in 1803. Johann Gottlieb Fichte wrote a systematic and idealistic plan in 1807. Friedrich Schleiermacher responded to Fichte in 1808. Still others, including the central player – Wilhelm von Humboldt (a renowned scholar who was well-placed politically) – wrote short, less philosophical pieces.

This was a moment when some people had trust and hope in philosophers to lead – to lead with ideas. Germany yielded many idealist philosophers. The idealists articulated a certain kind of hope for philosophy and for higher education, often in conflict with the church and settled power structures, including the landed gentry. Schelling and Fichte were like celebrities. Their lectures were well attended, their books widely read. Each in his own way explored the unity of all knowledge and offered highly metaphysical accounts of the world (and of education). Up until then, philosophy had struggled to gain firm ground within the university, free from religious, political, and economic interference.

The ideas of critique, unity, and academic freedom are grounded in these struggles, and I revisit them not to document what these philosophers thought but to revisit the role of ideas in the research university.

Some of these philosophers' models and ideas for universities still hold sway, and recent debates about critical thinking and academic education are deeply connected to these earlier, more philosophic, debates.

Thanks to his inside-track position, Humboldt's plan won the government's approval, and to this day his plan constrains what is possible in our research universities. But my focus here is Schleiermacher's model. Even though his plan did not prevail, it contains the seeds of current universities' aspirations and limitations.

From 1808 to 1810, Humboldt was the government's secretary for religion and public instruction. In this role, he argued for the connection between research and teaching. Indeed, he claimed that when a researcher professor lectures before students, the professor learns both by framing his thoughts to communicate them to the students and also by answering their questions. He extolled the benefits of research, but he was most interested, in today's words, in the creation of new knowledge.

He argued that the progress of science would be slowed or even blocked if researchers stopped teaching.

In the ensuing two hundred years, many universities adopted Humboldt's principles and even some of the practices of his model. It's clear how professors can benefit from this model, but the benefit to undergraduates and, more importantly, the goal of their education is less certain.

Humboldt's protégé, Friedrich Schleiermacher, was the secretary of the small committee that made the final proposal for the university to the Prussian government. He had published *Occasional Thoughts on Universities in the German Sense* in 1808.[1] Although his model was not accepted, he became rector of the new university and set out to implement Humboldt's model. Schleiermacher was a leading romantic theologian, the "discoverer" of the concept of religious experience, the founder of hermeneutics (the science of interpretation), and a translator of Plato. He was someone keenly interested in language and communication and shared that interest with Humboldt. He oriented the University of Berlin toward a synthesis of the mathematical sciences and what we today call the humanities.

But let's look at Schleiermacher's rejected model. Almost two centuries later, his model can help us understand the tension between research and undergraduate education in modern universities. Moreover, his account of education was an eloquent articulation of critical thinking. Students would study how we know and probe the limits of our knowledge. The university was neither the place where all knowledge was gathered nor the place where new knowledge was produced – it was the place where students learned how to test knowledge, to submit what is claimed elsewhere to critical scrutiny. As Schleiermacher states:

> The business of the university is this: to awaken the idea of science in the better young people who are already equipped with information of many kinds. To help it [the idea] to rule over them in the area of knowledge, to whichever each wants to devote himself, so that it will become their nature to regard everything from the viewpoint of science, to look at everything individual not for itself, but rather to examine it in its

> closest scientific connections, and in a great combination bringing it into stable relation to the unity and totality of knowledge, so that they learn gradually to work out for themselves through this faculty, in every thought to become conscious of the fundamental laws of science, and, to research, to discover, and to display it.[2]

The goal of the university, according to Schleiermacher, was to aid the student to see that all knowledge needs to be made systematic or unified. A large gap exists between the knowledge or information that one first learns and this later idea of science. The university is not where one practises the inquiry of science but the place and time of awakening. Schleiermacher laid out the consequences: (1) students must gain a lot of knowledge before they come to university, and (2) truly productive research does not belong in the university.

Schleiermacher identified university education as training to recognize the unity and the limits of our knowing, or, in shorthand for philosophers, transcendental reflection. University education is a kind of metaknowledge that evaluates and unifies all knowledge claims. It focuses on what makes knowledge possible (How can we know?) more so than on the information we do know (What do we know ... ?).

To isolate the specific task of university education, Schleiermacher separated three types of thinking into three different institutions: (1) schools, (2) universities, and (3) academies. Academies are sometimes called associations or even institutes, such as France's National Centre for Scientific Research (CNRS) or the Princeton Institute for Advanced Study. His account of knowledge and the tasks associated with its progress allowed for this separation. University education fell between helping individuals obtain knowledge (in schools) and developing knowledge (in academies).

Schleiermacher referred to knowledge as *Kenntnis,* which could be translated as "information." The task of the university in his view was neither to transmit nor to produce information but to train us to interrogate and integrate information. Libraries and the huge data capacities of universities are therefore secondary or subordinate to the task of education. Librarians are not merely guardians of information but rather reflective and supportive of critical reflection and research. The accumulation and management of information support the critical insights cultivated in university.

I take the term *Kenntnis* to indicate what we would call *settled knowledge*, such as a tradition, and it is bound to the idea of knowledge. In its substantive form, knowledge is, if not permanent, at least stable and defined.

Study in this idea is acquisition and accumulation; it is *having* knowledge but also being formed by learning a tradition. It takes many years of schooling to acquire sufficient knowledge of settled matters. If you look at a basic-skills approach to education, or even a mathematics curriculum, you will see the cumulative way each year builds on the previous one. Controlling a lot of knowledge or information is certainly part of secondary education. But what role does knowledge play in higher education?

THE IDEA OF KNOWLEDGE. Knowledge is completed information, that is, knowledge that is settled, stable, and defined, if not permanent. For students, learning knowledge is acquisition and accumulation; it is *having* knowledge but also being formed by learning a tradition.

Schleiermacher devoted the university to the idea of critique. He portrayed university education as helping students negotiate an adolescent moment (*Übergangspunkt* or "transition point") when the acquisition of settled knowledge in school turns over into the production of knowledge. The decisive moment occurs when everything a student has learned is joined in a profound unity. To the extent that university education is not simply advanced high school, it requires moments for interrogation and exploration to disrupt the assumptions and methods that underpin our settled knowledge. This unsettling or disruption is the idea of critique.

THE IDEA OF CRITIQUE. To explore how we know by probing the limits of knowledge. Students learn how to test knowledge, to submit what is claimed elsewhere to critical scrutiny. Critique is to think in the present; it focuses on self-conscious reflection in science.

The questions that arise during critique do not lead to settled knowledge being thrown out but rather reorganized, allowing some of its closed sets to become open ones. Schleiermacher referred to this process not as acquiring more knowledge but rather as "learning how to learn" – though I hesitate even to write this well-worn mantra. Here, what the students are learning is not more information but how to explore the question, What makes knowledge into knowledge? They become the knowers and not the receivers of knowledge, and this thinking makes the knowing happen in the present.

I do not discredit the idea of knowledge. My point is that, for the founders of the University of Berlin, the goal of university education lay beyond that idea. One can still find apologists for universities as places that teach settled knowledge, people who praise a certain image of the liberal arts and sciences. Henry Newman's *The Idea of a University* is often marshalled for this purpose. Often, this is a "great books" version of education; occasionally, it's a defence for moral education in the form of enduring (or even unchanging) virtues.

It seems appropriate, then, to illustrate the shift from the idea of knowledge to the idea of critique by considering the study of Virgil.

For many, the greatest literary work of the Roman Empire is Virgil's *Aeneid.* Consider Bernini's sculpture of Aeneas, the hero of *The Aeneid* (Illustration 1). Aeneas is a Trojan soldier who fled the conquered Troy near the end of the Trojan War (twelfth century BCE). Here, he's carrying his father, who carries the household idols, and he also brings his son. As immortalized in Homer's *Iliad* and *Odyssey*, the Greeks won the Trojan War and wiped out Troy. Aeneas, a survivor, escapes and manages to make it to the shores of the Tiber, where he conquers the Latins, eventually leading to the founding of Rome.

Here's a concept of heritage, of transmission, of translation from Greek into Latin, from a past world into a new present. Aeneas saves what matters most, his father and the idols, for the sake of the future (his son). Here is a past he cannot leave behind without leaving himself behind. We are, in other words, in a relation with the past. (Compare this to the modern story of progress, which upholds science and technology, invention and resource extraction as our saviours. As if they'd save either Troy or its memory.) Is this what we do in the university, especially in the humanities? Do we save classical cultures and their values for the future, to teach our children to be virtuous?

Virgil's story is about needing the past. The humanities seem to cling to this story; we carry it in our moments of crisis. Within this story,

1 Bernini's sculpture of Aeneas, Anchises, and Ascanius, 1618–19

knowledge and tradition serve an idea of knowledge as that which is already known. In contrast to the fast track of commercialization, the university serves as a reliquary. The ancients are fixed, even eternal, and wise; they stand in opposition to profit, with "future impact" counting as the only justifications of the "enterprise" called "the university." But bearing this settled body of knowledge is now no longer a plausible task for the university, even for the humanities.

So here I pause to draw attention to this account of Aeneas being not a Greek image, or even a Trojan image, but a Roman one. This is the story the Romans told about their ancestors, and through this telling, they reframed their heritage at the moment their republic changed dramatically and uncontrollably into an empire during the first century BCE. Few classicists can tell the story of Aeneas carrying his father and the gods without recognizing the critical impact of Virgil's telling on Roman history and our own as we retell the story of Virgil or the story of Gian Lorenzo Bernini sculpting Virgil in the early seventeenth century.

For Virgil, the future of Rome was its unfamiliar breaking with the republican past, so he wrote to stabilize the Romans' past. But the role of Virgil in our own past is also unstable. Would we be here if the British had not elevated Virgil in their own dreams of empire? Here, we see the idea of critique at work in the humanities: this idea destabilizes the Trojan past, the Roman past, and the modern European imperial past, and we can discern all of these disruptions by studying older texts. These texts are household gods (or idols); at each turn, they articulate the need to face the uncertain future by drawing on a somehow fungible past. We reread; indeed, we teach students to read to learn something different from the past and the retellings of the past, from the history of the retellings. The humanities do not carry the past like an object, even a divine object – they study the texts to reset them in new contexts, in circles of tellings and the contexts of those tellings, bringing them forward into our moment, just as those tellings had been brought forward for the anticipated futures creating our present moment. We make the past remarkably unstable.

Destabilizing through layers of tradition and by jumping from context to context represent critical reflection on how we know, and that reflection unsettles knowledge. Literary history, as pursued in the university, is not limited to the transmission of eternal beauty and truth, where the aim of instruction is to develop and improve the student.

The more common justification for humanities departments in fact challenges this idea of knowledge with the ideas of critique and inquiry. Indeed, the uplift or edification of founding stories without critical reflection can limit and perhaps mislead students. Universities are not running Sunday schools to indoctrinate students in a tradition (even the tradition of radical politics). Rather, they teach students to question how the past is used and reused and how the "greats" have been made great by readers to serve other purposes. The social or political history of Rome is studied in the university not to transmit knowledge of the past but to interrogate it and to help students discover that the need to create imperial history is perennial, particularly in times of regime change and global ambition. Retelling the origin of the Roman Empire illuminates the origin of the British Empire and, indeed, the American empire.

The student learns to think and evaluate in the present moment of thinking. Thus, to shift from the founding of empire (which is, perhaps, not our own present) to the decline and fall of empire, we might look to Apple TV's 2021 adaptation of Isaac Asimov's *Foundation*, itself written in the 1950s in response to the two world wars of the twentieth century and with Edward Gibbon's eighteenth-century history, *The Decline and Fall of the Roman Empire*, sitting on Asimov's desk.

As a vast technological and political empire collapses, how can we save the culture, ideas, and values we cherish? To make sense of the almost apocalyptic experiences of the present, we must study not only science but also history and literature, all with the idea of critique.

This sense of the present, the moment of knowing, is also characteristic of modern science and its self-conscious subjects, who learn to know by making present to themselves what others had known. The authority of the present, of the student's own thinking, is awakened and unsettles tradition, even if it resettles it. The idea of critique is not simple, but it does tend to emphasize the student's agency in thinking now over the authority of the past.

This idea of critique appeals to university students because it makes the university the site for contesting past knowledge (what they were taught growing up) and for attending to the call for change. The challenges of the excluded and the oppressed, of those made invisible and unheard, can alert us to what could have been otherwise and to knowledge deemed necessary in its time. It is a characteristic of students of the next generation to doubt and criticize the past. In waves and intersectional planes, the university cultivates those who question the economic dominance of small elites, justifications for slavery, the exclusion of women, traditions of racial hatred, and critiques of critique itself, which serve to constrict access to privilege and education.

In our time, we see these battles in bold relief and bitter shame in relation to Indigenous peoples and their knowledge. The great classical texts are a heritage of Western imperial hegemony, so we can question them. Critique does not mean discarding the past, but it can mean challenging it, and standing in judgment. Universities are profoundly ambivalent places: on the one hand, they encourage critical reflection on society and its past; on the other, they have been vital to European colonialism, undermining traditional knowledges and implementing technologies and economies that excluded – and, indeed, murdered – many people and cultures. Tradition and settled knowledge are suspended in a present moment of questioning. Do we need to study Virgil to learn piety or, rather, to help us question the image of a rising Rome after the fall of Troy?

Whereas critique was the hallmark of university education in Schleiermacher's model university, research was the purview of research academies and institutes, places where mature scholars develop new knowledge and new methods, write books and articles, and participate in the scientific community. In Schleiermacher's day, institutes did basic science research or compiled large archival historical projects over dozens of years. Much of the great historical and philological work and many scientific discoveries and advances happened in these research societies and academies.

It still does. The European Organization for Nuclear Research (CERN), the Max Planck Institutes, the CNRS in France, the National Institutes of Health, National Research Council Canada, and many others are publicly chartered and funded research institutions. Their task is not to teach students. They do not, in other words, help others obtain knowledge, nor do they teach others how to engage in critique or even inquiry. They research. Focusing exclusively on research is a fantasy for university faculty who wish to be left alone to do their own work or, at least, who pursue teaching releases to work collaboratively with other faculty. Schleiermacher himself was located much of the time in an academy even as he explored and then helped construct a university.

Thus, for Schleiermacher, the research academy was a place where the idea of inquiry guides thinking, which was not the business of students. These academies would, supposedly, have genuine independence from economic forces and state control, because he felt academic freedom was crucial for discovery. Research would be ongoing, requiring longer time frames. Whereas the university cycled people through learning the logic of inquiry, the research academy hired them for decades to pursue new knowledge.

Schleiermacher's university for critique was open to anyone who qualified in the schools. He expected the university years to be few (compared with schooling years and research years). The university would be a sorting place where most students would learn how to learn about one field. The majority of students were not destined for a life of discovery and research, but they could learn enough to respect the real scientists. They would learn new ways of thinking and find their vocation as professionals or, in many cases, as members of the civil service.

> **THE IDEA OF INQUIRY.** To discover new insights, invent new techniques, and create new laws and new ways to renew our society.

Schleiermacher made a strong case that the university-educated would be much better qualified to hold civil service jobs. He foresaw a better-educated ruling and managerial class, a class allied with and respectful of science, a class able to fend off fanatical religious leaders and the wealthy propertied ruling classes. These students would have enough experience with inquiry and questioning to engage with the knowledge attained in schools as they practised their professions and altered or discerned the limitations of established protocols. Schleiermacher's vision still describes most of the undergraduates in our universities – people who have learned to learn and can keep learning after they graduate.

A second group would learn in a more profound manner and become the scientists and researchers of the academies, who would dedicate themselves to discovering new knowledge as their life-long career.

An even smaller group would get stuck in the university as the professoriate. This third group would be qualified to do scientific research, but it would be only a small part of their work. For them, teaching would be primary.

For those of us who have become professors, the goal of higher education is to stay in university for all our years – but it's hard to say that undergraduate education has the same goal. One of the first memorable pieces of pedagogic advice I received as a graduate student teaching a course was *not* to make it into the philosophy course I wished I had taken. Why? Because few, if any, of my students would likely end up as philosophy professors.

In Schleiermacher's model, the person who aspires to stay in the university to do research is an outlier. Only a few graduates remain at the university – scholars who wish to guide others through this transition. Their vocation is not to teach students settled knowledge but to challenge them and teach them how to criticize knowledge and, if possible, to teach a few of them to discover new knowledge. They train real scientists and scholars to move into the academies. Reproducing the professoriate is a very small component of their mandate. The university, for Schleiermacher, was a distinctly philosophical or metascience place. "Real" researchers went on to the academies, but the university's professors were the masters of critique, people who served that idea even if they mastered information and conducted their research on the side.

The Future

With help from Schleiermacher, I've distinguished two kinds of learning for university students: (1) learning knowledge as a tradition and (2) learning how to criticize knowledge. In the first, the past is dominant because settled knowledge forms the students. In the second, the present reanimates past information, guiding students to know in their present moment.

Will critical thinking make the future already knowable in the present? Does this model form students and their future lives to goals they already know in the present? A research university needs to make studying about discovery and creating new knowledge, about creating a future. It would focus on what is not yet known – the work that Schleiermacher consigned to research academies and institutes. Our students need to learn to think in ways that meet and, more radically, create the future. We need a richer account of the future, one that moves from a future that is simply the present over and over again, through a future that is something that emerges as if by necessity from the present, to a future that is so radically new it can't be reduced to a necessary, deterministic unfolding of the present.

Such a future is intrinsic to inquiry and is also, I would argue, at the heart of any system of ethics or even a social theory.

To help us explore this future that university graduates could create, let's look at a specific turn in European philosophical thought – the turn away from the present of the self-conscious subject to a future of possibilities.

If the nineteenth century began with a flourish of idealism during which philosophy was invited to step onto the world stage, then the mid- and late nineteenth century closed with turmoil from failed revolution and Germany's ongoing struggle between traditionalist Catholics, liberal rationalists (often allied to materialists and proponents of the new science), and older propertied conservatives.

This turmoil led to a nineteenth-century version of the culture wars. In the strangeness of enemies and allies, Hermann Cohen (1842–1918), a Jewish philosopher, was appointed professor at the University of Marburg in 1876, in part to score against the Catholic party. Cohen was one of the few Jews appointed to a university anywhere at that time. His role in philosophy and the Jewish intellectual world is a topic for a different book. In short, he weathered violent storms of antisemitism to fashion a system of philosophy that was widely influential across the intellectual world.

Cohen was the leader of a school of thought that renewed Kant's philosophy of critique. Cohen championed the future as the key to understanding research and, indeed, to understanding human existence. His system promoted examining existing knowledge to discover how we know and, more importantly, to propel our thinking into the future. We should reflect critically on the sciences (natural and human) and religious and cultural texts to see where new insight is needed. In the process, we'll learn that the process is more real than any result can be – because science goes beyond knowledge by seeking new laws, new experiences, and new institutions.

Cohen's philosophy is, in short, a logic of inquiry. To sustain that logic, he altered our familiar account of time by putting the future first:

> The future contains and unveils the character of time. The past entwines itself on the anticipated future. It was not first: rather the future is first.

> The past arises from it. In the face of the not-yet the no-longer emerges ... Where then does the present remain, that one takes care to regard as the fixed point? It is no less than this: it hovers in the row that is made up simply from those points: it occurs in the hovering between the anticipated future and the catching up, the fading, of the past.[3]

This is not simply a claim about the nature of time. Rather, this is about the time of thinking – of science, ethics, culture, and religion. We create modes of time for our world, and the future is first. Cohen even argued that the study of history is structured around the future.

The "not-yet" that guides our efforts to know and act became a constant refrain of many thinkers in the twentieth century. Although their thinking took distance from Cohen's, they recognized that the past depends on the not-yet of the future, and the present hovers between them. This future, moreover, arises in judgments of possibility.

The work of research is a kind of searching within the realm of the possible that allows us to advance knowledge. We begin with what is already known. We then question the known in a mode of critical reflection and, on that basis, through research, we open new possibilities for the discovery of new laws, things, cases, individuals, and emotions. Cohen wrote:

> The work of Research: ... *possibility* marks the relationship to research. The judgment of possibility smooths the disposition for the beginning and the approach to scientific research. Critique is necessary here at every turn, and not only negatively; rather extensively positive ... Thus it can be explained that in this region, the judgement of possibility has marked out the universal concept of pure knowing, and the founding of a specific meaning, for the development of research: the hypothesis.[4]

Cohen wrote about research and inquiry as ways to seek out new laws and new individuals.[5] Knowledge is not merely what is already known, nor is it knowing what is already determined and will be completed in the future. Cohen showed that we seek to know a world not yet established according to laws, laws that are also "not-yet." Critical reflection does more than lay foundations under current knowledge: it opens up new inquiry.

But this call to the future still requires engagement with the past. For Cohen, the present is yet to be fulfilled or perfected (either morally or in terms of knowledge), and the past did not have to be as it was. The world has not been redeemed – many are hungry, suffering, and oppressed, and we are destroying the earth. The work of critique disturbs the temptation to study in order to justify things as we find them by claiming that they must be so.

Nor should we look to the past as an ideal, as a time when everyone was treated with dignity, when wisdom and knowledge were complete. The judgment of possibility also allows for a critique of history, the removal of fatalism or determinism, which allows for the discovery of a wider range of options in the present.

Today, we fear the return of war, the exclusion of women, the rule of the unaccountable rich, the surge of hatred, and the destruction of the earth and all who live on it. But the future is not sealed, and our present does not have to be as it is. Possibility is a richer category than necessity, and it reflects our finite world.

But can the university increase the range of possibilities for its students? Examining Schleiermacher's model of a university for critique – a model not adopted – helps us understand the limitations of the dominant model of the research university. We can see how some ideas might be blocking us from teaching students to inquire.

Today, the undergraduate years often provide a grounding in settled knowledge while professors are pressured to pursue new knowledge and status for doing important, groundbreaking research. Both of these poles are contrary to Schleiermacher's vision. His university for critique unsettles our knowledge and our history. His layering of knowledge, critique, and inquiry follows from the linked, tense relationships among these three ideas. Each institution – the school, the university, and the academy – depends on the others in some ways, but each also contests the others by defining its activity as the most profound. Schleiermacher could argue for the inherent value of each activity and, thus, for the government's need to recognize the public good that each institution pursues. All pertain to epistemology, addressing their own kind of thinking and their own kind of learning. Each makes its own claim about its purpose – the essence of the university being education and other activities.

But we can't help but notice that Schleiermacher's model university professor is the sort of educator we see less often now. For Schleiermacher, a professor who is interested and capable of doing ongoing intensive research, who wants to pursue new avenues and discover new knowledge or cultivate new interpretations, would not be a professor. That person belongs in a research academy: "Assuredly we have two very different occupations here: the academic in solitary meditation pondering all the available findings, using all suggestions, and thus advancing new discoveries, and the university teacher always moving around within the same circle, living with youth eager for knowledge and stimulating them in all kinds of ways."[6]

Perhaps we see here the ongoing effects of Schleiermacher's translations of Plato. Plato was Socrates's student. Socrates did not write, he did not set up an institution, but he was remarkable for his critical inquiry. His questions forced people to learn that they did not know what they thought they knew. A Socrates rarely produces another Socrates, but Socrates succeeded in producing Plato and other participants in philosophical "research" or exploration. Socrates did not engage in research, but he obsessively questioned and challenged settled traditions and knowledge. His student Plato founded an academy where he taught, expounded on new knowledge, and maintained ongoing inquiry.

Did Plato understand his work as a sort of new inquiry that was producing new knowledge? Or did Plato understand his teaching as truly Socratic, that is, appropriate for only a short sorting period in a student's life? Was attending Plato's academy a short intervention (the way the experience of Socrates often was), or was it an occupation or even a profession?

We might ask this about university teachers: should they do research? But first, let's pause to think about the development of the mind. How does a person learn to explore and create new knowledge? If we consider adults learning languages, we can see that someone must first acquire knowledge about the alphabet, vocabulary, and grammar. This knowledge precedes expressing yourself fluently in a new language. And that fluency then allows one to question the inflections, grammar, and specifics of a language to ask second-order questions about learning languages.

In other words, control over information is a condition for critical reflection. But beyond reflection lies the creation of new meanings in a language: both in the form of literary creativity and translations into and out of the language. Here we see beyond the idea of critique to the idea of inquiry. But are the questioning and the exploration of new knowledge sequential? Is the idea of inquiry distinct from the idea of critique?

Here, then, is the moment to add a timely comparison. It was Humboldt's less-developed scheme that specifically challenged separating research from university education. Moreover, he challenged this separation on the very grounds that Schleiermacher preferred: on the practice and progress of knowledge. For Humboldt, too, the communication of knowledge was intrinsic in knowing, and even more so in the discovery of new knowledge:

> If one defines the university for only instruction and dissemination of knowledge, but the academy for its extension, one commits an obvious injustice. Knowledge has been advanced as much – and in Germany, even more – by university teachers as by members of academies. And the university teachers have made these contributions to the progress of their disciplines precisely through their teaching appointments. For unconstrained oral communication to an audience, which includes a significant number of minds thinking in unison with the lecturer, inspires those who have become used to this mode of study just as surely as does the peaceful solitude of a writer or the loose connections of an academic community ... It would be entirely safe to entrust the growth of the sciences to the universities alone, as long as they are properly ordered, and for this goal the academies can be dispensed with.[7]

Humboldt refused to separate research from the university and thus helped create the profile of the professor not merely as an instructor of settled knowledge but as a true leader in discovering new knowledge.

In short, Humboldt rejected the claim that the professor and the researcher were two different types of people doing different types of thinking. The irony is that, although Humboldt's vision resides at the centre of almost all research universities, the focus today is on excellence in research and the cultivation of professors who are more talented in the laboratory and library than in teaching undergraduate students. When the undergraduate curriculum is a complex body of basic science or a sequence of great books, it's very hard to connect research excellence to undergraduate teaching.

One of the contemporary symptoms of this division is that research universities have confronted the problem by doubling the stream of professors. Research stream professors are expected to teach less so they can focus on conducting research and inducting a smaller number of students into that kind of thinking. Teaching stream professors are assigned to do a great deal of teaching, often in large classes, and are usually expected to have a smaller research profile, sometimes restricted to researching how to teach university students.

It should not surprise anyone that teaching stream professors are sometimes exceptionally talented and creative teachers who often create undergraduate curriculums that include research. But they are often lower status in their departments, and some departments and faculties have resisted having such streams – out of a certain kind of loyalty to the ideas of Humboldt. Insofar as today's undergraduate programs are focused on critical thinking and the research professors are diverted from teaching undergraduates, the model being followed resembles Schleiermacher's even if the self-description seems closer to what Humboldt proposed.

Humboldt argued that in explaining advanced knowledge, the professor would begin to see new paths forward. But then, he went much further:

> One unique feature of higher scientific institutions is that science always deals with a not yet fully solved problem: this means it remains always doing research. The lower levels of education present closed and settled bodies of information. The relation between teacher and student at the higher level is a different one from what it was at the lower levels. At the higher level, the teacher does not exist for the sake of the student; both

exist for science. The teacher's business depends on the students' presence and would not take place without the student.[8]

For Humboldt, science required the copresence of teacher and student, who together advanced science in its searching in relation to the idea of inquiry. The researcher-as-professor was more likely to have had his horizons disturbed and new directions and new knowledge instigated than a pure researcher.

What emerges in Humboldt's plan for higher education is tension about the place of research, but it also eclipses critical reflection for those who do not go on to do research.

Schleiermacher recognized a specific educational activity for those students bound for the civil service and the professions. However, it's not clear that the scholars working in isolation (communicating with each other but without the cyclical engagement of teaching new students critical reflection) would produce the same intensity and quality of new knowledge. And we could ask both models whether professional schools should also be teaching students how to do research.

By using Schleiermacher to pull apart research and critical thinking, we can see how they could come together in other ways. If the idea of critique and the idea of inquiry are not identical but offer different and perhaps even competing tasks for higher education, then we may need to assess the effect of combining them in one institution. Clearly, one must learn much knowledge and also learn how to criticize that knowledge to shift to the future. Even in Schleiermacher's plan, there's some seepage between the three activities.

But we can also recognize that sequence is not the same as fusion. From the idea of knowledge could come an institution devoted to learning settled knowledge or tradition. This might well be the familiar claim about the liberal arts and some colleges. (Here, again, I mention Newman as one of this model's champions.) Arguments for universities as places that develop citizenship sometimes lean toward critical reflection on settled knowledge (more like Schleiermacher's model); at other times, they lean toward studying tradition to gain enough knowledge to assess the claims of politicians and media. Moreover, as I show in Chapter 3, we must also recognize that changes brought on by information technology dramatically challenge the role of the idea of knowledge in the university.

For my purposes, however, while both Schleiermacher and Humboldt recognized the student's need to have learned much knowledge (and even to learn some knowledge at university), the central task of the university is found in the dialogue between critique and inquiry. My challenge is to switch the focus from the professors' capacity to that of the students. If universities combine these purposes and functions, we must reflect on what would constitute a theory of thinking and what sort of intellectual biography would suit today's students and, indeed, the work of the professors. University education is a kind of learning that goes beyond instruction at school, regardless of whether it combines with research.

Schleiermacher elevated the idea of critique for most students, while Humboldt saw undergraduates contributing to the professor's exploration of new knowledge. Cohen propelled beyond the foundations and unity of science into a future that does not yet exist. And Humboldt cracked the door open to this future with "a not yet fully solved problem." But here we wish to fling the door wide by going beyond the need for students to learn new knowledge from others to explore the capacity for them to discover new knowledge.

For Schleiermacher, research should happen outside the university. If researchers seek only to advance knowledge, then, in his view, they should not be professors. For Humboldt, students were valued for their contribution to new knowledge, but the modern research university pays limited attention to educating undergraduate students not bound for research careers. Schleiermacher was tempted to borrow from the medieval guild pattern, in which undergraduate students would be like journeymen trying out for the guild of researchers. (In which case, the PhD, or perhaps better, the publication after the dissertation, known in the German world as the *Habilitationsschrift*, would qualify one to become a master and permanent scholar – that is, tenured.) In each case, there's a gain for science or scholarship, for knowledge and its progress.

I certainly don't want to stage a claim against that noble idea, but I also wonder if we can focus again on the middle activity – the critical reflection or, if you prefer, the questioning of settled knowledge and traditions. There is a risk that this middle activity will simply be dropped out – to go directly from acquiring information in the mode of high school students to discovering new knowledge as researchers. What Schleiermacher discerned is that we need a critical turn, a moment of discontinuity, to turn the settled past into an open future.

Learning how to reflect critically is an opportunity to offer present challenges to the past, to accentuate the present moment when the student is thinking. It is obvious that the accumulation of information – more data, more indoctrination in the settled matters of the disciplines – is not conducive to creativity. The future brings both opportunities and challenges, calling for new inquiry and discovery. Today's students are of necessity facing that future through climate change, wars, social injustice, and economic uncertainty. Undergraduate education could be that moment when all knowledge is suspended and viewed from a new angle. It might be that binding this moment of critique more tightly to as-yet unknown knowledge, the discovery and invention of researchers, may create a slightly different loop, but the research university can't abandon that moment to become society's research and commercialization labs.

Schleiermacher's model should lead us to demand an educational justification for the university's extensive research activities. While the discovery of new knowledge, the exploration of new technology and new social practices all are good, it's not obvious why they should happen in the university rather than in separate institutes, societies, or academies.

Instead, I propose that a stronger justification can be found in the argument that research should be the core of a university education – that students are in university to engage in research or, rather, to learn how to do research. Any account that simply regards students as aids for the professors to advance knowledge is not adequate. What I seek is a way to make research contribute to the student's education or even some sort of curricular integration of research into their education.

This idea presumes that students would benefit from their education revolving around research. This is not Schleiermacher's model, nor is it Humboldt's (with the exception of graduate students). It is not at all what drives Newman's idea. My hypothesis is that we need to ask, How can universities teach students to pursue new knowledge? Here, we're moving beyond the necessary stage of critical reflection and, indeed, beyond teaching students how to learn new knowledge as it emerges in their lives. Guided by the concept of the future put forward by Hermann Cohen, I'm asking if we can teach students how to discover, create, or invent new cases, new things, and new laws.

Schleiermacher challenges us to think about learning how to learn, of learning for the sake of critique. This reasonably leads to a familiar concept: life-long learning. The sense that new knowledge is being discovered, new problems are finding new solutions, and new histories are challenging our venerated traditions – this understanding points to why a person would need to learn not just once, as a youth, but would need to keep learning, to change with changes in technology, political action, social relations and, of course, the massive problems we're experiencing today.

Learning the logic of inquiry – that would prepare students to be the creators of new knowledge. They would become the ones to write the new histories, to produce the new policies, to invent the new technologies, to address the profound problems that will develop in the future. Their future would no longer be to learn their whole life long but throughout their life, to create a future – an unexpected future.

2

Multiplying Inquiry and Innovation Beyond the University

Rabbi said:
Much Torah I learned from my teachers; and more I learned from my colleagues; and from my students I learned more than from all of them.

– *Babylonian Talmud,* Makkot 10a

Our small workshop collapsed.

Department chairs, a couple of vice-deans, and a handful of PhD students had been meeting for a full day of a two-day workshop to discuss how the University of Toronto's world-class PhD humanities programs were working. Our focus was the future careers of students. Over the course of the workshop, the graduate students offered less and less, until they almost fell silent. At that time (and things have not gotten better), most PhD students were ending up with jobs that did not look like their professors'. Some were doing other kinds of jobs in universities, such as in teaching streams or administration (in so-called alt ac or alternative academic positions) or working as postdocs running labs. Others were teaching in secondary schools or working in the nonprofit sector, government, industry, and so on.

Our topic was how to adjust our programs to reflect these "unexpected" outcomes. One story stood out. One student reported that professors regarded students who did not get teaching jobs as failures. She said she knew of a student who asked for a letter of reference for a desirable government job only to be told by the professor, "I'll write one for you for this job, but I will never write one again for you for an academic position." None of the professors in the room expressed surprise, much less disapproval.

At the end of the day, the students asked to speak alone with me, the convener. They said the workshop was not working, that the professors simply did not listen to or respect their concerns. They already knew that their desire to question and explore what the PhD was for was unimportant to the professors in their departments, but they also saw evidence of their lack of interest at the table. They did, however, want to keep meeting, and they hoped the Jackman Humanities Institute would host and listen to their concerns, which we did.

The professors presumed people acquired a PhD only to become a professor, but students wanted to explore how programs could be adjusted to support other jobs, including the professions and vocations.

How can we understand these students' concerns? And how can we place PhD students and their education at the centre of the research university, where all the students are learning the logic of inquiry?

That failed workshop happened in 2013, midway through my term as director of the Jackman Humanities Institute. Soon after, I received an invitation to participate in a discussion about the future of the humanities PhD from Paul Yachnin, who was directing a new humanities centre at McGill, the Institute for the Public Life of Arts and Ideas. The discussion expanded into a series of activities, grants, and projects that struggled to take up a fundamental conundrum: most of the PhD students in research universities did not end up becoming professors at research universities.

From our positions outside the structure of humanities departments and arts and science faculties, we directors connected with various deans and vice-deans of schools of graduate studies and explored the situation both within and without the humanities. There had been a massive expansion of PhD programs in the 2000s, so there were concerns that students could not find university employment because the market was saturated. Administrators were shifting their focus of concern from the university's cost for the extended time it took to complete a PhD to the question, Where does a PhD student find employment?

Many institutions (including the University of British Columbia, the University of Toronto, the Council of Graduate Schools in the United States, the Ontario government, and the Conference Board of Canada) tried to count where PhDs were going, and the results were striking. Almost all PhDs ended up with jobs within a few years of graduating, some in sectors that were high-paying and intensively research-oriented (especially in the natural and biological sciences). Approximately one-third end up moving into the ranks of professors. This is considered a high success rate, but it means that approximately two-thirds do not end up as professors. Alas, the situation was more critical because the attrition rate of people who enrol in PhD programs is approximately 50 percent. So, of the students who enrol in a PhD program, half do not complete their degrees, and only one-third of the half that do (on a fairly optimistic reading of the data) become professors. In short, five of every six students who enrol in a PhD will not end up a professor in a university.

The problem is that for the most part, and overwhelmingly in the humanities, the goal and measure of success in a PhD program is to become a professor, which means that five out of six doctoral students fail – leading to the presumption that a student who considers employment outside the university should be cast off.

If you know PhD students, it will not surprise you to hear that this stage of their education is not often happy. It can take six or eight years to finish a PhD and another ten years to adjust to a "failure" to land a job as a professor.

Our group did not discover this problem: people had been writing about it for over twenty years. But we did further the conversation about how to re-envisage PhD programs by taking into consideration alternative career paths for the PhD. Since that time, PhD programs have shown some recognition of and at least some preparation for these alternative paths, provoking some of us to think a bit more about learning outcomes. What does a PhD student learn? And how can a PhD help you play a role in society beyond the professoriate?

Replicating or Multiplying

For this chapter, I want to start with the dominant model in the research university: the research university as a replicating organism.

PhD education is bound to the idea of replication. At the core of this idea is a general theory of power and self-preservation (turned into power over others and ultimately over the future) that follows a debatable philosophical axiom: all things desire to remain in existence and reproduce to extend or sustain themselves in existence. Things reproduce by creating replicas, or repetitions, of themselves. Such an idea seems plausible for almost any institution or system. Because the university tries to remain, or survive, as it is (or even as it once was), it struggles to make the future more of the same – not really a future, not an open future at all. According to this idea, university professors aim to reproduce by replicating themselves in their students.

THE IDEA OF REPLICATION. Reproduction by replication means creating replicas, or repetitions, of oneself. For the university, the goal is persisting or surviving as the university is now (or even as it once was). University professors aim to reproduce by replicating themselves through their graduate students, who will become professors.

Without getting too graphic, we can readily see that PhD students are an instantiation of the idea of replication. I hope my PhD student will live on to continue my work and in some key way replace me as a professor in a university. Again, one could interpret a business, a farm, a law firm, or a presidential (or prime ministerial) dynasty in the same axiomatic form.

So how does this idea of replication guide education in a research university? I might begin, as a professor, seeing teaching as getting the student to know what I know or perhaps to think as I think. If I assume that I have knowledge and maybe the royal road of methods for creating more knowledge, then I do not merely wish to impart my knowledge – I want to cultivate a replacement, for I must, at some point, retire. I might even want to raise a school, a group of people who, as professors, continue with my method or engage the truth, as I see it.

The idea of self-sustaining reproduction produces a view of science that is deeply conservative: even if knowledge is not already settled, there should be strict continuity along the path we're set upon. This view conforms to what some have called "normal science." From generation to generation, teaching will continue, and students' minds will be formed to imitate the teacher's. If we apply this idea to undergraduate research programs, we'll select only the very best (or at least those most devoted to the idea of inquiry as embodied in professors) so that they, too, can eventually become professors.

What I propose instead is to turn the university upside down – that is, inquiry should flow from the undergraduates to the graduate students to the professors. If the goal of replication is to generate flow from the top, from the professors down to the undergraduates, then this inversion requires a new idea, which I call the idea of multiplication. In this upside-down model, PhD students undertake an enhanced role in teaching undergraduates the logic of inquiry. They teach undergraduates to seek new knowledge in unanticipated ways. In the process, the PhD students learn how to teach others the logic of inquiry – a skill that is itself valuable beyond the university.

The modern PhD owes a great deal to Schleiermacher and Humboldt because it became a focus of the University of Berlin, from where the degree spread to other universities over the next two hundred years. Within that Berlin vision of the PhD, the idea of critique and the idea of inquiry were connected (with a bit more emphasis on critique). Recognizing that the focus of today's university education is distinct from acquiring settled knowledge, we can see that the PhD tightly links critical reflection (which unsettles knowledge) with inquiry (which leads to new knowledge).

THE IDEA OF MULTIPLICATION. In multiplication, we have responsibility not only to ourselves or another person; we are also responsible for other people's responsibility to others. In a university setting, this means attending to other people's intellectual capacity to attend to other people's intellectual capacities. In other words, a professor is responsible for what a PhD student learns and for the students who the PhD student teaches.

The degree itself, the doctor of philosophy, is bound up with the idea of critique. To gain a PhD is to have learned how to teach this critical aspect of reflection, in whatever field. One does not get a doctor of chemistry in chemistry but rather a doctor of philosophy in chemistry. The PhD is not merely expertise in a field but rather mastery of thinking that is reflective (and so seems like philosophy). Because the goal is to educate those we hope will become our replicas (the professors who will be our successors in the universities), we devote time and resources to our PhD programs and confer academic status by measuring our students' success at replication (read: placement at research-intensive universities).

Because there is no need to create a mass of professors, and since the vast number of undergraduates will not become professors, the idea of replication provides no reason to teach undergraduates the logic of inquiry. Many universities do have programs in which elite undergraduates can learn how to do research, but only a few students are put on a track that could lead to a PhD and a vocation as a professor. This is a recruitment model or, indeed, a replication model, for only a select few undergraduates.

Our devotion to the idea of replication comes at the cost of most PhD students and almost all undergraduates. To begin to make sense of what our current practices are and what the innovations should be, we need new ideas about the goal of education in the research university. If the goal is teaching the logic of inquiry, as I argue, we can begin to meet it by building into PhD programs education that enhances their capacity to lead and teach others how to inquire. The professor's role is to teach the teachers: to educate PhD students to pursue research while listening and cultivating the questions of the undergraduates who they are teaching to research.

This idea of multiplication offers us a notion of reproduction complicated by ethical responsibility. The idea I'm sketching here concerns time and the relations among the generations – a challenging theme developed by Emmanuel Levinas (1906–96). Levinas was a leading figure in French philosophy in the latter half of the twentieth century. He, in turn, drew on a tradition reaching back to rabbinic Judaism (200 BCE to 600 CE). Excluded from the university until his mid-fifties, Levinas played a key role in the French Jewish community as the principal of a Jewish teacher-training school for several decades. Even as he wrote major philosophical essays and books, he continued to teach teachers, and one of his major innovations was introducing the study of traditional Jewish texts. My sense is that Levinas's contribution emerged from the confluence of his philosophical expertise, his practice as an educator, and his recovery of Jewish thought for our time.

Levinas used the term *fecundity* to link teaching with ethics. Teaching does not simply add one more person who now knows the truth – it engenders the responsibility of that person to teach others. Teaching is not simply a matter of addition or supplementation. I've named this idea *multiplication* to capture the radical increase in learning that follows from it. For Levinas, fecundity concerns the multiplication of the ethical responsibilities one has for any other person. He drew on images of teachers and students and of parents and children. He noted that "the biological origin of this concept [fecundity] does not in any way neutralize the paradox of its meaning but delineates a structure that goes beyond the empirical biological."[1]

The contrast between the idea of replication and the idea of multiplication – both of which are central in evolutionary biological science – gives us a clearer view of teaching and intergenerational ethics. Empirical biology finds both ideas in play: replication is at the core of genetic mechanisms; multiplication speaks to a wide variety of processes, particularly in mitosis and meiosis and the way that cells and organisms reproduce. In biology, replication and multiplication are connected closely, but in the world of universities, and, indeed, in many institutions, a gap can be opened between the ideas. Discerning and widening this gap could transform our universities from providing a university education to an elite group to a much larger number of students.

Universities do not confine themselves to transferring knowledge; they are engaged in teaching students to question and to inquire. Because of this, we must reflect on the purposes of learning, and of ethics. University education, ethics, and communication interact and form a matrix in the task before us.

Levinas is often grouped with the dialogical thinkers (Buber, Marcel, Rosenzweig, and so on). The premise here is that thinking happens with more than one mind and that knowledge depends on some sort of dialogue or interaction. Thus, to get a sense of what the idea of multiplication promises for education, we can sketch the arithmetic of responsibility and consider a mathematical progression of ethical responsibilities.

1 *Responsibility for one.* If my core ethical responsibility is to care for myself, then knowledge will be based on self-knowledge, and education will be a process of learning how to know myself, even if that self is not something fixed but changing or growing.
2 *Responsibility for two.* According to Levinas, I'm responsible not only for myself but also for another, for the person who faces me. This seems dialogic, but it does not need to be reciprocal. I'm responsible for someone else regardless of how he treats or regards me. Learning, then, becomes a relation to another who I never fully know and who is not a mere extension of myself or under my control. This other person has something to teach me. This encounter with another person breaks up my own habits and my self-relation and creates the learning situation.

   Here, we break with the axiom of self-preservation (that things must always act to ensure their existence) and with an analytic of power. I cannot control the other person, but I'm still responsible for him. Moreover, Levinas argued that the other person addresses me, calls me to speak, and so resists my power but not with a counterforce. Language is capable of enforcing power relations, but it begins, Levinas said, with vulnerability and a call to attend to another person. To respond to this call is to be responsible. This experience of learning from another focuses on me giving an account of myself and being open to new insights from another.
3 *Responsibility at a higher power.* I'm not only responsible for the other person but also, in a reproduction of responsibility, I'm responsible for the responsibilities that person has for other people. I'm not only responsible for my child but also the responsibilities of my child. Thus, if she undertakes an obligation, I'm a surety. Her responsibility to feed a hungry person becomes, in my relation with her, my responsibility to see that she feeds the hungry one. Here, we see that responsibility extends far beyond what we can control, indeed, beyond the horizon of my agency or power. We are not merely responsible

for each other but for each other's responsibilities for each other. This is the relation of multiplication.

In a commentary on a subtle Talmudic text ("The Pact," *Babylonian Talmud, Sota* 37b), Levinas explored how the formation of a true community depends on many commitments or obligations that form covenants or, we might say, treaties.[2] While the context of the passage from the Talmud is not simple, Levinas presented the commentary at a colloquium addressing the theme of community. The Jewish community in Paris was struggling to recover from the Shoah, and Levinas was leading a series of annual colloquia. For many years, he would introduce an opaque Talmudic text to address Jewish intellectuals who knew about everything except Jewish texts.

The Talmud itself arose as a product of schools of study during the rabbinic period (200 BCE–600 CE). The Talmud is a set of commentary texts written in many voices and devoted to exploring disagreements, and it is studied in Jewish academies and schools. The Talmud was a response to the calamity of the Roman destruction of the Second Temple in Jerusalem in 70 CE and then persecution and exile under Roman authority. Israel had quite limited political sovereignty, but Jewish communities now became minority communities in the diaspora without armies and with limited jurisdiction. Without a Temple, there was no longer a role for priests. The canon of the Bible was fixed and prophecy ceased.

The rabbinic sages of the Talmud replaced the priests, the prophets, and the political rulers – and elevated the practice and theory of study. Their texts, moreover, have become the cornerstone of the surviving Jewish communities. Levinas devoted much of his life to leading Parisian Jewish intellectuals back to those texts and the work of study, repeating the traditional Jewish pattern of responding to disaster with study.

The hero of this extract from Levinas's text is a later sage, Rabbi Rav Mesharsheya, from the end of the fourth century CE. In this passage, two scholars are having a dispute, and Rabbi Mesharsheya resolves it by articulating a fundamental distinction: "It is the difference between responsibility and the responsibility of the responsibility."[3]

In other words, one can be responsible for everyone in society, or everyone in society can be responsible for each other, but there's also the possibility that one can be responsible for other people's responsibilities. Levinas commented: "One is not only responsible for all of the others, one is responsible for the responsibility of all of the others. One must thus multiply 48 by 603,550 and again multiply the product by 603,550."[4]

The numbers reflect discussions that led up to this climax in the text. Forty-eight represents multiple commitments made over time in the biblical narratives; 603,550 is the number of Israelites wandering in the desert. Hence, responsibility for everyone's commitments is the product of the number of commitments each person has undertaken multiplied by the number of people. But Levinas argued that this product is multiplied again by the number of people because each person in society becomes a surety for each and everyone else's responsibilities for the responsibilities of all the others. Each person is responsible for everyone else, and each is also responsible for everyone else's responsibility: "This is extremely important. We just saw something that resembled recognition of the other person, or love of the other person. To such a degree that I am surety for the other person, for the adherence and fidelity of the other person to the law. His concern is my concern."[5]

We can imagine that the second level of our ladder – responsibility for the other, or for two – resembles recognition or even love of the neighbour. But it is the third level, where the number of people is raised to a higher power, that generates a surfeit of responsibilities. This magnification of responsibility exceeds my own projects and my own power and, indeed, my own survival.

I only gesture to the extremity of Levinas's ethics. In the next paragraph, he adds that there's no end to this increase. What I'm hoping we'll gain from this idea, however, is a social vision with interconnections that markedly exceed the simple exchange or self-interest.

This idea of multiplication offers us a way to think about the relations between the generations in education. How can understanding our layers of responsibility help us understand the task of university education? Has something been increased, some aspect of education that is not simply the pursuit of power and control over other people and, thus, the future? Even when we add the continuing replication of the teacher, is this not simply some other mode of ongoing control?

For Levinas, the key was to think about our children. Children are more than a continuation of their parents; they are a new beginning and a future beyond the parents' control. Responsibility dislocates us from ourselves into a future beyond ourselves. The other and the others for whom the other is responsible are not in my control, yet I still bear responsibility for them. Do we teach only to instill our knowledge in others and to prolong ourselves? Or is there a promise of new learning and discoveries in our students beyond what we can foresee? Is this not a source of hope for the future? And is that hope also not the university's assignment?

The idea of teaching students how to learn and to discover new meaning and new knowledge exceeds replicating the past into the future. The idea of inquiry orients us to the future, but we can now begin to see that students can lead the work of research. If the professor can attend to the capacity or even the responsibility of inquiry in the PhD student (that is, engage in careful supervision), then couldn't the PhD student also attend to the capacity of inquiry in undergraduates? Instead of telescoping to find the few undergraduates capable of research, we might focus instead on multiplying the number of people learning to do research. This multiplication will take us from learning how to learn to teaching the teachers, who will teach all of the students how to seek new knowledge. The future that opens here is replayed and multiplied in our PhD students when they act as teachers, when they are called to open the logic of inquiry not only in themselves but in their students.

With this vision in mind, the question becomes, How can teaching responsibility of this sort help frame a model for the research university?

Configurations for Teaching Research

Earlier, I mentioned that in my role as director of the Jackman Humanities Institute, I sat on many committees. In some ways, this book emerged from what I learned there. One committee, Academic Policy and Programs, reviews reviews of programs throughout the university. One year, I found myself reading the review of the psychology program at the University of Toronto Mississauga. I'd been wondering, How could we build a curriculum around teaching students, all students, the logic of inquiry? Unexpectedly, I found a long shout-out for a method in a review of the program's first-year psychology lab.

The students involved in the lab were not the crème de la crème of undergraduates. Rather, almost fifteen hundred students each year learned how to do research. The program had a computer lab with eighty stations, and there were eighteen sections (or seminars). The students learned the basics of research and ethics, followed a cookbook lab, and then designed their own instruments to sample and crunch data and write it up. The lab instructor, Jeffrey Graham, had designed the lab and software and supervised the corps of psychology graduate students who taught the first-year undergraduates the logic of inquiry.

This course inspired me to look far and wide for models of teaching the logic of inquiry at scale. Of course, ornery critics will note that most of the questions these students pursued were already familiar and that this was not groundbreaking research. But the actual goal or "learning outcome" was for them to learn the thinking that is research. They had to lead the inquiry, not merely follow directions, to examine their own questions. Without the graduate student leaders, the lab would not have worked. The leaders, in turn, learned a great deal about how the logic of inquiry is learned.

Here, I'll sketch six configurations to help us think about how we can teach students how to do research. Each of these configurations already exists in our universities, if implicitly. But the opportunities to coordinate and expand these configurations to institute change are often blocked by limiting ideas such as replication or knowledge that, in different ways, obscure students' capacities to contribute to research.

In the strongest configurations, we find the multiplication of research as PhD students learn by teaching undergraduates the logic of inquiry.

This teaching occurs in lecture halls and classrooms but also in laboratories and libraries. Some classes have laboratory sessions; some students are key players in research laboratories. I'm interested in how inquiry and knowledge flow between people in these settings. My diagrams are almost like cartoons, but they can help us find our way to interrogating the task of PhD education in relation to the idea of multiplication.

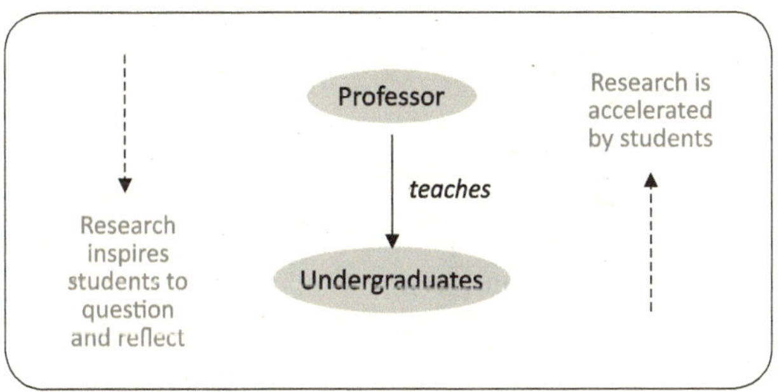

Configuration 1

Configuration 1 involves a leading research professor lecturing undergraduate students on settled knowledge in her field and recent advances in research, including her own. This model represents the Berliners and the long-standing tradition of lecture courses. The lecture content can be new theories or scientific claims, but it can just as well be a humanities scholar's new reading of a traditional text.

PhD students are absent in this configuration. The professor benefits from teaching, and the teaching moment may do more than inform the student – it might make them want to engage in research like the professor's. More than a tourist, the student is seriously engaged in the questioning that created the context for the professor's research. But the student learns in a way that is still close to "schooling" with its focus on acquiring information, even if the lecture pushes the student toward critical thinking.

We can see here that teaching augments research and the progress of knowledge. In addition, students learn more than updates about research discoveries and trends: they see how research provokes the reflective thinking proper to university education. The professor's new inquiry is made to challenge settled knowledge. But the students are not yet learning the logic of inquiry.

Configuration 2 modifies the situation by adding the PhD student. We now have three relations, and the fulcrum is the PhD student, who mediates education from the professor to the undergraduate. This can be a lecture class with sections led by PhD students. In the sections, the PhD student leads a seminar-style conversation.

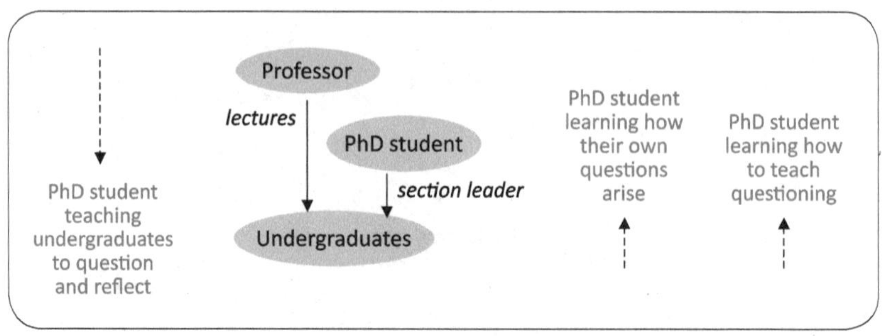

Configuration 2

This learning configuration can be more than a mere information transfer from the professor, who has the most knowledge, to the PhD student, who has much knowledge, and the undergraduate, who has less knowledge and is coming to acquire more. Teaching critical thinking here means teaching students to reflect on methods and ways of knowing; it's about the unsettling or opening of knowledge.

So beyond imparting settled knowledge, what does the PhD student do? As a mediator, her role is to aid the undergraduates to learn to reflect and to question in a challenging way. Indeed, because the PhD students are closer than the professor to the undergraduates in terms of their knowledge and culture (and also closer to the shock of experiencing education as critique), they are more likely to teach undergraduates questioning and reflection. Their task is not so much to transfer knowledge but to engage them by unsettling established knowledge.

But what does the PhD student learn by doing this activity?

Of course, the PhD student is taking courses, working in labs, or pursuing her "own" work. But her teaching role can also further her PhD education. Thus, in this configuration, PhD students learn how to teach reflection and questioning (not merely delivering information). One can imagine the PhD student benefiting from the professor's master knowledge – knowledge about how to teach, how to develop critical thinking in an undergraduate student, which would, in turn, help advance the PhD student's capacity to question and think.

But learning can also flow in the other direction. In the discussion section, undergraduate students engage with lectures or readings with greater licence. The PhD student learns more about the task of teaching from what has and what has not worked for the undergraduate students in the professor's lecture. While the undergraduates are learning how to reflect through critical reflection, the PhD students are learning from the undergraduates about how reflection arises and what aids and/or hinders such thinking.

But there's no attempt to teach undergraduates the logic of inquiry, to learn how to do research. The PhD student becomes more aware of her own interests and resistances. Education becomes a second-order event as the PhD student learns about the path of learning in this way. Whether the professor is learning in the same reverse flow is another question, but it's interesting to see that the PhD student, working as a TA, is not only serving the purposes of undergraduate education but also gaining an education at a second order.

Here, we get a glimpse of the idea of multiplication. Learning how to teach allows the PhD students to become responsible for the undergraduates' education in service to the idea of critique. But because the professor is responsible for the course, the professor is also responsible for the responsibilities of the PhD student. The professor is teaching the teacher. Importantly, the task for the professor is to attend to what is in some ways beyond his control: the PhD student's teaching. If the university conducted no research, the capacity to educate in the specific sense of this critical and reflective thinking would still follow the idea of multiplication. Graduate education would accentuate the idea of critique precisely by attending to how the undergraduates take up this thinking.

This might be the place to emphasize that these configurations are, if not ideal, at least abstract. The features I'm describing are unevenly achieved in today's classes, but these configurations could be used to justify the PhD students' role in the university – as more than apprentices or replicas of researchers. They could also be used to justify better funding for these new roles, providing an incentive for professors to engage PhD students in these ways.

PhD students, however, are also engaged in research. The point of their degree is that they are being taught how to do research, which is, of course, a series of practices but also a way of thinking in the search

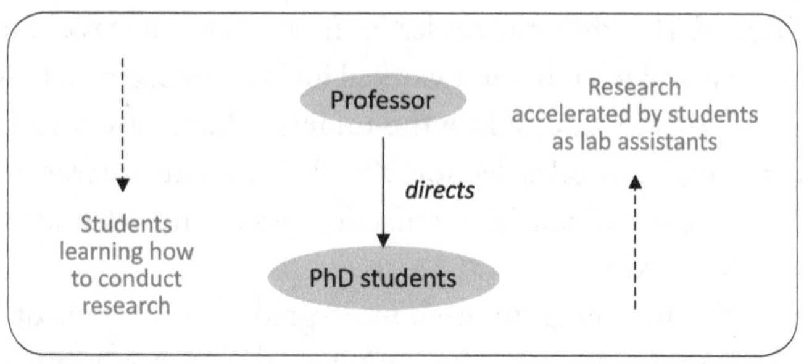

Configuration 3

for new knowledge. Configuration 3 is a research laboratory with a professor and PhD students.

This context often includes postdoctoral researchers (*postdocs* for short). Postdocs are a group that few people have addressed in thinking about universities. They could play an important role in the flow, on the one hand, leading questions from students into the research and, on the other, helping teach PhD students and undergraduates the logic of inquiry.

From this point on, as we'll see, my account becomes even more cartoonish, but configurations help accentuate areas that need more thinking. One sort of configuration has a principal investigator, a professor who secures a research grant to explore a project of interest in a field of their expertise. The task of inquiry requires several levels of support from other people, people who run experiments, program computers to collect and organize data, evaluate results and adjust the hypotheses, or help organize the people and equipment. We might ask, Which of these tasks is research? The likely answer would be that all of these tasks are research and that the laboratory works because everyone's activities in the lab are coordinated. But what is the specific role of the PhD student in the laboratory? Or, more significantly, How does he learn how to do research?

Whether in a wet lab with test tubes, materials, animals, and so on or a dry lab with computer-assisted configurations, much of what is learned is hands-on, much like an apprenticeship (or perhaps, more accurately, a journeyman's work). People are learning from other people in physical proximity, and the PhD student is advancing in the task of framing a hypothesis, designing an analytic process, building the equipment, collecting the data, interpreting the results, and writing it all up. Developing the capacity to undertake research, to seek to know something that is not yet known, requires not merely curiosity and intelligence but also discipline and method – all in a practice-based context for learning.

Some laboratories are designed to teach the practices of inquiry in a clear and stepwise manner. Only the professors bring the questions, and each step reflects the participants' progress through the graduate program and intellectual range. The person one step up from you guides you in learning your current step. Inquiry emerges from a socially and intellectually disciplined ordering. It can often be the case that the postdocs are just one rung up from the dissertating PhD student.

I would not equate this simply with an industrial or manufacturing model – the practices and tasks of the PhD students may, indeed, be the key to learning how to investigate new questions. Nor is this simply schooling in the sense of distributing information: at each step, participants learn a new stage for seeking knowledge. Unlike experiments with known processes and results, this is a living lab that can produce unexpected results and frustrating failures. The practice of inquiry includes dealing with the difficulties of what is not yet known. There are stages to envisage before and during research – and people attend graduate school to learn in these stages. In such a configuration, moreover, those above are responsible for those below. The PhD student's role reveals that graduate education intrinsically includes learning how to do research, how to seek new knowledge or a new view on settled matters. The university is not itself producing new knowledge but teaching people how to inquire.

But a research laboratory in a scientific research institute might not include graduate students or even postdocs. It might serve the idea of inquiry but with the task of teaching removed. The PhD student learns information new to him but only as much as is needed for the work of discovery. Of all the students at the university, the PhD students are the ones who would seem to be most focused on learning how to do research. Thus, for many research universities, the expansion of graduate education

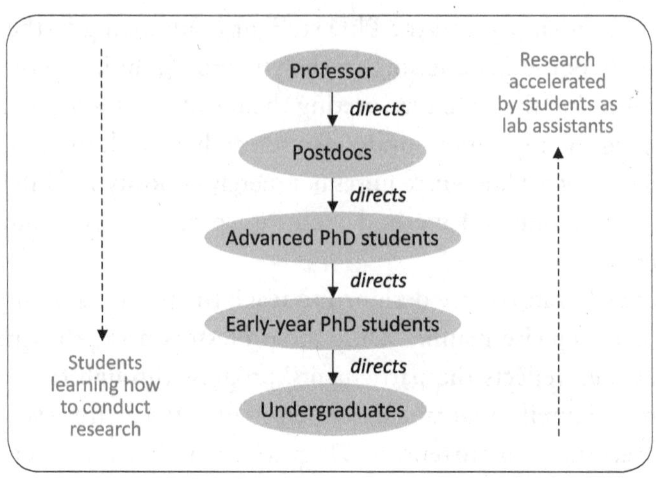

Configuration 4

is essential for the university's research capacity – both in terms of people and resources. A research academy is free from the challenge of teaching graduate students how to do research, but it also lacks people to staff the lower steps on the ladder.

Let me now add undergraduates to this laboratory. In Configuration 4, we have a true pyramid: one professor, a few postdocs, several dissertating PhD students, several early-stage PhD students, and a gang of undergraduate students (we could add master's students too). Undergraduates occupy the bottom step, which can mean their tasks and their learning are primarily mechanical or labour-intensive, for example, cleaning, preparing equipment and materials, and recording data.

In such a configuration, two issues are brought into focus: (1) the undergraduates are not doing research, but they are learning something about a specific social organization for producing research, and (2) the PhD students are, in relation to the undergraduates, primarily taskmasters and instructors. Here we have the whole guild hierarchy: masters (professors), journeymen (PhD students), and apprentices (undergraduates). If we add in the postdocs, the undergraduates simply become the servants of the apprentices and journeymen.

Teaching the logic of inquiry and creating new knowledge is segregated near the top. The premise is that control of information and critical

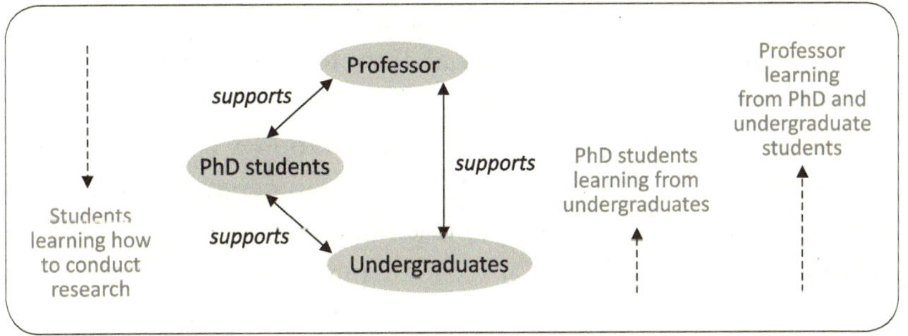

Configuration 5

thinking are preliminary to research. Even if everyone works in the laboratory together, segmentation is unavoidable, as this social ordering reflects. Standing on a middle step allows a person to better understand the social and intellectual sequences and modes of integration. But graduate education assumes one will ascend the ladder.

Configuration 5 includes undergraduate students focused on their learning how to do research. Such a lab would encourage a series of research projects, and each member in the lab would pose their own questions. The flows of inquiry would be even more multidirectional.

The PhD students are learning how to support other people's research, not simply the professor's project. The less experienced, less expert undergraduates also need support and guidance. But the tasks are not clearly segmented, so the gaps between each rank are less obvious. Nonetheless, we can see that PhD students can guide or mentor undergraduates because of the proximity of experience and culture. The goal, moreover, is to help develop the logic of inquiry in the undergraduate.

We have arrived at the turning point – for the first time, the research capacity of undergraduates comes into focus. I'm not proposing that PhD students be nursemaids or janitors for undergraduate students in the lab. On the contrary, both kinds of students are learning new abilities and insights that do not appear in these diagrams. Undergraduates are learning the basics of running a research organization, but they are also learning how to move from questioning and reflecting on settled knowledge to imagining and exploring new knowledge and discovery – from the idea of critique to the idea of inquiry. The undergraduates are, in fact, positioned to learn how to do research and are learning that by doing it, as was the case in the University of Toronto Mississauga's innovative first-year psych lab.

Much as the session leaders in Configuration 2 are learning in a complex way as they teach critical reflection to undergraduates, the PhD students here are learning how to teach others how to do research. In addition, they are learning – at second hand with the undergraduates around them – how new projects accumulate, grow, encounter obstacles, and require revising. Guiding others to do research is not the same as learning how to conduct it yourself. PhD students reflect and gain insight into how knowledge engages with the matter under investigation and how a person's mind can expand and change in this process.

It is the close proximity of the laboratory that offers these higher-order insights to PhD students, preparing them to become professors who will teach the next PhD students and guide research inside the university and out. They are learning how to be teachers of inquiry. (The professor, for the record then, is responsible for undergraduates learning how to do research and PhD students learning how to teach someone to do research, a specific responsibility not always included in current laboratory research.) In some cases, the best experiments will come from undergraduates, in others from PhD students, and in many cases, from professors, but the university's interest is in helping the undergraduates learn how to conduct research and in teaching the PhD students how to help them.

If Configuration 4 moves the undergraduates stepwise into the laboratory to prepare them by having them play a role in research, then Configuration 5 accentuates their research capacity, creating new hybrids of education and research. The professor's research and its goal of discovering new knowledge take place in a context where student learning is turned toward what no one knows yet. PhD students play a key role in this configuration: their graduate education is focused not only on their own research but also on guiding undergraduate research. Here, we have genuine multiplication: the research and education of the other person is, in fact, a task. The future is multiply embodied in the various kinds of students, and the responsibilities to teach and to learn abound.

Let's turn to one last configuration. Configuration 6 presents a non-

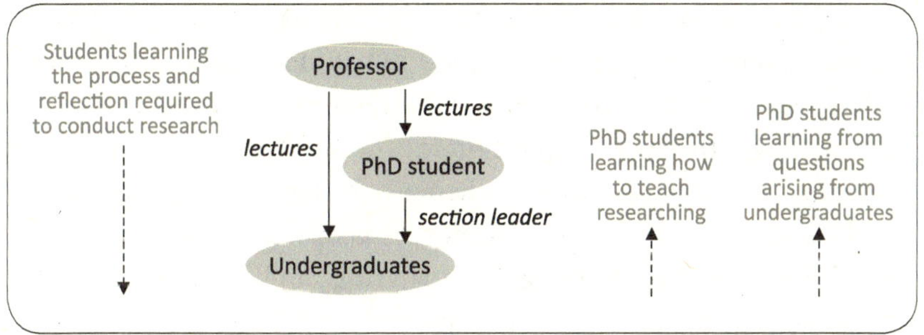

Configuration 6

laboratory context, a classroom in the humanities, to see if it's possible to move beyond the critical thinking of Schleiermacher's model of the university: to look for undergraduate students learning how to do research. We can imagine this scenario either with PhD students or professors leading the class, but the key issue is the moment when we bring learning how to do research into this classroom. How can an undergraduate learn how to do research in a seminar?

In the classroom (versus the library), there are more peers and less time (versus the lab) to engage with one another daily. But in the classroom, the tasks of research can also be explored – from framing a question, to designing the steps for the inquiry, to collecting the materials and analyzing them, to writing it all up. In humanities courses, this last task is the research paper, through which students engage with contemporary or older but prominent canonical texts, cultural events, or interpretations of a question. In the social sciences, students and researchers engage with contemporary theories and policies and bring in an original claim. Undergraduate research is not often earth-shattering. For the professors, it may feel more like an exercise. But the goal is to learn how to do research: how to question and reflect on settled matters and how to engage in inquiry that will lead to new interpretations and new insights.

In the context of PhD education, the PhD student faces an added challenge: writing a dissertation. They engage in research at a more mature and thoughtful pitch, but at the same time, they learn how to guide undergraduates in their first runs at framing and writing a research paper.

Just as I try not to presume that every undergraduate student wants to become a philosophy professor, the PhD student does not teach an undergraduate how to write a dissertation but rather a paper or an essay. At every stage, the specific question for inquiry has to come from the researcher: they alone have the challenge of bringing it into focus, defining the scope, and deciding what more is needed and what can be discarded. These ways of thinking and analyzing can be learned.

When learning the logic of inquiry and how to do research, the flow must go in both directions, to and from undergraduates. The PhD student engages in second-order reflection on the challenges faced by the undergraduate student and learns something about the new questions that arrive with a new generation.

The question is, Can this configuration address the crisis in replication?

A Society with Questions

To capture what's at stake for PhD education and the research university, let's add one more twist. In this dialogue between the idea of replication and the idea of multiplication, we can contrast two kinds of tasks for the university, yielding a way for education to contribute to research beyond the university.

The focal point of replication is the professor's research – which represents the very progress of science – and the goal of PhD education is to create the next generation of professors. In periods of expansion, replication requires a greater than one-to-one relation; in periods of contraction, professors oversee fewer PhD students, and the students' research is closely framed to replicate the professor's. There is an almost tidal motion here in the tension between teaching information and the desire for new knowledge. The dissertation is not viewed as an especially significant contribution to new knowledge but rather represents the completion of training in doing research. In theory, the next research project will secure the new professor's tenure (much like a masterpiece that comes after the journeymen's work), replacing the professor.

The idea of multiplication, by contrast, emphasizes the capacity and creativity of the next generation. The goal of education is to teach others to do their own research and also to teach PhD students how to teach undergraduates how to do research. This second-order learning is not simply learning how to become the professor – it's learning how learning how to do research happens, and the professor teaches the teacher. It's the reversal of the proverb "Those who can, do; those who can't, teach": "Those who can research, do; those who can do research better, teach (others how to do research)."

Thus, multiplication presumes a vested engagement in cultivating curiosity and the rigorous and reflective work that is research. The research university cultivates the undergraduate's research capacity and the PhD student's research capacity and ability to teach how to do research. The professor does her own research but also has the responsibility to learn from undergraduate and PhD students. Questions for research come from all sides, and the professor has multiple goals: to produce many important publications and to graduate two groups of researchers – those who have learned how to inquire (undergraduates) and those who have learned to conduct research and to guide and to teach others how to do so (PhD students).

Research often occurs in settings independent from the university, and higher education can occur in educational institutions and settings separate from the research university, including apprenticeships in trades, technical schools, and professional schools. These various kinds of learning are not all suited or necessary for every person, and they do not need to occur in every institution. It may well be that not everyone needs to learn how to do research. In places where research occurs outside the university, the focal point is either new discoveries, the production of new bodies of knowledge, or new products for the market.

We could follow Schleiermacher and consign the appropriation of information and traditional knowledge to high schools, and assign education in critical thinking – with its reflection, disruption, and insights – to an American-style liberal arts college or even a small university whose primary goal is not research. Students would learn to interrogate settled matters and tradition; they would learn to reflect on how one learns. This university would not focus on how one discovers new knowledge or new interpretations or on the PhD student learning how to teach others to inquire in a research mode.

That said, if we are trying to justify the education of all students attending a research university, then it seems we need to grasp how the research university can educate students as researchers. We could start by confronting the crisis we're facing today: our universities have become massive. Their capacity has expanded, and they educate many times more students than fifty or even fifteen years ago. Is it reasonable to expect that we can educate tens of thousands of undergraduates and educate them for research?

But starting this way, it seems to me, is putting the cart before the horse. The real question is, What is the goal of a research university education? If we imagine a flood of students learning how to do research, engaging in inquiry to produce new knowledge, to find new solutions to new problems – well, we might just have the beginning of an important justification for undergraduate education in a research university.

This requires us to see the future as one where the people who can learn and discover and discern matters that are new, who can engage with changing situations, are highly valued.

Let's call it a society with questions (not a knowledge economy).

In a society with questions, premium value is placed on people who can inquire because the challenges of meaning, technology, justice, sustainability, and security require new questions and new inquiries, not merely the dissemination of current knowledge. A society with questions is one where the future is open and where the university helps hold it open. It requires people schooled in more than long traditions or those who have learned established scientific knowledge.

The prospect of mass university education is promising. We would be tapping into the questions and intelligence of a much broader range of people. But it raises questions, including how to educate for this outcome, a question that governs the rest of this book.

If we focus on the education of researchers, we may well see PhD students serving as double agents: learning how to do research and serving as the undergraduate's guide to research, they might develop into more reflective and subtler researchers. (And we might also redevelop what we expect for and from the postdocs too.) I'm suggesting, under the idea of multiplication, that we recognize the doubled-ness of PhD students to enhance their role in educating other students.

This idea is not easily articulated in our current system, even when it's occurring. So to describe this role for the PhD can seem like loading yet another major task on the TA, who might already feel burdened and distracted by their teaching work. Still, this path could offer a richer range of careers for PhD students. In the lab or classroom, they can demonstrate their ability to manage a group and lead them in seeking new knowledge to address our world's questions.

But this would require a change of vision (or, dare I say it, ideas) for university education. In this vision, paying careful attention to undergraduates learning the logic of inquiry trains PhD students and even ultimately professors, yielding a large corps of people who can work in many sites on society's pressing needs.

The current desire to expand the teaching stream in universities reflects a desire to transform education away from the traditional notions of status. If we can offer something better for many more of our students, PhD students and undergraduates, paying attention to this upside-down flow may become even more viable.

The research university's current size and traditions make it hard to imagine professors working closely with all the students in an expanded undergraduate cohort. In a small liberal arts college or a university such as Oxford, it is possible to have one-on-one tutorials, a superior mode for critical education in which everything the student knows is subjected to scrutiny and reconstitution. (And it's this intimate education that would supposedly justify the much higher costs of tuition – and not student life outside the tutorial ... as I'll discuss below.)

But to learn how to do research requires more people than the professor, especially in the sciences. I would like to be clear that having PhD students help constitute research education is not simply a money-saving device (PhD students being paid less than professors). Rather, it recognizes that education is not so much a step process as a process that draws on people at multiple levels of experience and maturity in thinking. It might be best to have each undergraduate work only with professors, but I suggest that there's some real gain in placing the PhD student into the mix – a gain for each member of the triad. And those gains themselves reflect something about the idea of multiplication – that the discontinuity of generations creates something better.

In our day, professors are largely baby boomers and Gen Xers, PhD students are often millennials and Gen Z, and current undergraduates had their early university education disrupted by COVID-19. These generations have different outlooks on questions for research and even the manner of inquiry. The regular discovery that there are gaps between generations makes education less a matter of transmission and more a discovery of the power and freedom of discontinuity. An undergraduate who sees a gap between the way the PhD student and the professor explain or correct or encourage has the freedom to pursue her own approach and enjoys a less subordinate relation to the professor (as does the PhD student).

Using the idea of multiplication, I've shown how to turn the research university upside down. Questioning and learning can be driven by the undergraduates even as they participate and are trained in the complex logic of inquiry. PhD students are the key to multiplication because they show that guiding others is intrinsic to the work of higher education – it guides them to their own questions and their discoveries.

In many ways, we are already teaching in this way (depicted in the latter configurations) today. But measures of status still focus the research university on the quantity and impact of the professors' research. Funding and authority follow status, so gaining administrative support for turning the university upside down would require overcoming established resistance.

An exclusive emphasis on professors' research obscures the research university's potential to educate tens of thousands of students to do research in so many places in our society. In today's jargon, the greatest knowledge transfer from the university to society is the graduation ceremony – it is the students who have learned how to seek out unknown and unseen matters who can make the greatest impact on our world. If their university years make a difference in their minds for the remainder of their lives, then science advances dramatically from our teaching, our classrooms, our laboratories, and our libraries.

3

Slowing Down Reading and Thinking in the Digital Age

Who knew that trolls and miners would arise from new technology to threaten our world? My friend Brian Cantwell Smith published a book about the power and limitations of artificial intelligence. We debated whether his title should be *The Threat of AI*, *The Promise of AI*, or the anodyne *The Future of AI*. He chose *The Promise of Artificial Intelligence: Reckoning and Judgment*.[1]

When I was celebrating at a birthday party with Brian, shortly after the 2016 US elections, I met Geoffrey Hinton, one of AI's pioneers. He explained that Brexit and Donald Trump owed their victories to Cambridge Analytica and that, as a result, many people would suffer and even die. You don't need me to survey the debate, primarily apocalyptic but occasionally hopeful, about the future of a society in which data is mined and trolls attack anyone they disagree with. The ability to disseminate and tailor news to the reader, to go well beyond digital manipulation to produce false images and false videos – this all seems to challenge our basic sense of knowledge and the task of learning how to discern truth.

New alarms were set off in 2023 with the rise of chatbots and their capacity to generate academic writing on any topic within seconds.

I'm no expert on information technology, much less AI, but AI prompts me, as a philosopher, to ask: How can universities address this crisis about what will count as knowledge in the future? Or, more precisely, What can our students learn to guide them in this muddled storm so they can help society?

Again, I'm not primarily interested in what professors will contribute by way of new inventions or new policies, or even in Brian Cantwell Smith's important insights into the deep structures of judgment and thinking. I'm concerned about what our research universities will teach, and to what end. You might be hearing that students won't need to write their own term papers, that they won't be able to read extended arguments, and that they'll simply outsource to AI most of what we've been asking of them in class. Information technology is transforming education, just as it is changing so much else.

Today's students are born digital. They access information continuously, in small and occasionally large pieces, often from many different sources at once. It's often not clear where authority lies: In an article they read online from a newsfeed? In a blog post by a friend? In a social media post from a star? In an email that got forwarded from one friend to another? And there are answers online for any specific question: How many people live in Ukraine? Who was the prime minister during the First World War? What does the term *postmodern* mean in Lyotard? Or what is the ancient Greek word for *idea*?

For many more complicated questions, there are answers to be found (correct or otherwise) through search engines or ChatGPT. Writing this book, I've made extensive use of internet resources, including my university's library, dictionaries, articles, and many suggestions from Google searches. I'm unsophisticated and tend not to use Web 2.0 capacities well. Despite the temptation, ChatGPT did not write any of this book.

But students are expert, creative, and socially connected through their devices. They have privileged access to a vast amount of information. By the time this book is published, there will be new ways to communicate and access content. But when I was writing, many of the students I knew were in constant conversation with their "friends"; following TikTok, Instagram, Reddit, and Snapchat; sending WhatsApp messages almost continuously; tweeting on X (formerly Twitter); reading and contributing to Wikipedia; and blogging news items they'd read on their feeds. If this activity isn't happening on their laptop, it's happening on their mobile devices.

This story is, I'm afraid, trite but not false. Universities and high schools are struggling to revamp the technological capacities of classrooms, and they are encouraging professors to use information technology, which is so natural and basic to students. Events overtook us during the COVID-19 epidemic, as almost all university instruction migrated online, and the challenges of social media nearly swamped the university.

The darker aspects of this story are now prominent and scary: our online searches and interactions, including buying books or shoes or games, are stored in search engines. Our email (or at least the metadata) can be accessed by government agencies. Carefully designed programs monitor our activities and inquiries and then, in clever recursive functions, provide us with information that suits us. The grand data about us is not readily accessible to students, but it is available to others whose goals might be beneficent but are more likely to be focused on exercising power or, in the worst-case scenario, cruel, manipulative, and vindictive. Machine learning is progressing rapidly with implications for the future of commerce, politics, and, yes, even in university education.

The university was seen for centuries as the repository for and guardian of information – *higher education* meant higher access to information. Information is now massively accessible. If the university exists only to warehouse knowledge and to transmit tradition, then it is doomed. But the university's inability to claim a near monopoly on knowledge doesn't make it obsolete. The focus must now shift to our second idea: critique. The university needs to replace the question of access to information with an emphasis on judgment and interpretation. Such a shift, however, does not often enough lead to the idea of inquiry. Which prompts the question, What will research look like in the new information age?

By now, I hope you're counting on the humanities to bring their skills and insights to bear on the new technology. Throughout this chapter, I place a greater emphasis on the humanities than in other chapters.

Although the information technology revolution seemed, at first, positive for the dissemination of knowledge, it has marked losses: loss of the goal of one unified body of settled knowledge and loss of a grand narrative justifying the university as a place where all knowledge can connect into a greater whole. In the face of the collapse of grand narratives of progress, many in the university are striving to restore one or another of those narratives to secure a future of greater freedom, greater productivity, or greater technological power. In contrast, most humanities scholars are interrogating and inquiring, asking questions with no expectation of a settled answer.

The Idea of Discord

To better examine conflicts about what knowledge is when the idea of unity no longer holds, I turn to an idea of discord, as drawn from the work of Jean-François Lyotard. If it came as a surprise that philosophers played a central role in envisaging the research university in the early nineteenth century, it may come as an even greater shock that the province of Quebec, in 1979, commissioned Lyotard, a French philosopher known for his writings on postmodernism, to report on the status of knowledge. In *The Postmodern Condition*, Lyotard recognized that the spread of digital technology had already disrupted the central stories that had made the university the sole court for assessing the truth of knowledge.[2] In other words, even before email, the web, social media, and artificial intelligence, people understood that data had begun to drive our society and that information could not be confined in our great libraries and learned institutions. Lyotard was not overly worried about the fate of universities, but he was a champion of what I'll later frame as an ethical task for the universities.

THE IDEA OF UNITY. To be or become one; holding diverse matters together in a consolidated and integrated manner. In the university, the idea that all fields and faculties should be unified, most often in a theory of knowledge or a shared foundation.

In *The Postmodern Condition*, Lyotard explores how we tell stories to make sense of the world. Under the idea of unity, we have a specific desire for a grand (or master) narrative to hold all of history together and, thus, to give a single reason for how society works. Each grand narrative presents a fixed conclusion and so closes off the future. Lyotard sketches three kinds of grand narratives about knowledge:

1. A traditional narrative identifies the speaker, the current audience, and those in the past we speak about: "We are the heroes of our own story."

2. A narrative of the right to knowledge asserts that all people should have access to knowledge: "We can enlarge society to unite all people through the knowledge of enlightenment we bring."
3. A speculative narrative claims that there's a deeper unity to all knowledge: "We can bind all knowledge together and so bind all people who know together with an idea."[3]

Lyotard argues that these three narratives and their direct descendants are no longer working – they no longer wield the power to integrate society or persuade people that we can make sense of history. As much as we might like to use a grand narrative to justify where we are in history now, these narratives are simply unsustainable.

Consider the first narrative. Even the resurgence of populism, which somehow identifies our generation with the great ones of the past, strains to hold together the range of information and society in a single narrative.

The second grand narrative (asserting the right to knowledge, a.k.a. the narrative of the Enlightenment) is intimately bound up with the modern state, the nation, and the formation of peoples. But the splintering of communities into regions and social groups isolated in alternative truths casts grave doubts on the power of science to draw society together.

The third grand narrative, which makes an argument about advancing science, is (no surprise) Schleiermacher's and Humboldt's. In this narrative, the university is the place where the sciences are united through critical reflection, revealing some higher truth.

For Lyotard, neither contemporary Marxist theories nor critical theory's grand narratives with their promise of emancipation work. Critics of Lyotard disputed his claims and defended the emancipatory grand narrative. Ideological critique, they argued, could be traced along a long narrative that, by dialectical turns, would lead to emancipation. But Lyotard criticized the idea that knowledge or theory should aim for a final, unifying resolution of conflicts because we no longer trust the unity of knowledge to liberate us. For Lyotard, knowledge was now intrinsically plural, so he rejected unity as a goal for knowledge. Instead, he claimed that conflicts and contradictions are irresolvable.

But the sciences, as projects of research, are still called upon to justify themselves (to secure funding and to satisfy peer review) through mini-narratives. Even without recourse to grand narratives, scientists explain their goals and results through local narratives. For example, health scientists justify their claims for new discoveries in ways that are different from how scientists justify discoveries in artificial intelligence, but both rely on mininarratives.

Lyotard claimed that the strongest forces threatening the task of science were demands for efficiency and a speedy return on investment. Scholars who develop local stories to justify funding often defer to an ideology of transparency and speed. Scientists can't justify their research through grand narratives but are expected to adhere to a set of rules or protocols to persuade a local audience of peers in their field.[4] This process is not arbitrary or relativist. In Lyotard's terms, it is pragmatics. Pragmatics is a component of semiotics, a theory of meaning that focuses on signs (including language). Pragmatics looks at how a person using a sign (speaking, writing, or reading) finds or creates meaning in relation to the sign. Pragmatics often focuses on context, on theories of action, and on personal pronouns, which show how *I*, the speaker, am implicated in an utterance.

As disturbing as his analysis was (it sparked a vigorous backlash against postmodernism and French theory, especially in the United States in the 1990s), Lyotard caused us to look more clearly at the work of justifying knowledge claims. The mininarratives, or local norms, are part of what makes each science, including the human sciences, truly a science. The relationship between research and critical reflection we explored in Chapter 1 is pervasive in the world of scholars and scientists, but the bases for such arguments are no longer universal.

The challenges to the second and third grand narratives are particularly disturbing, but forty years after the publication of Lyotard's report, they do not feel as transgressive as they once did.

For instance, the colonial imposition of Western science and culture throughout the world depended on colonial universities. These institutions delegitimated traditional kinds of knowledge and were linked to the practices of cultural genocide. A grand narrative about the advancement of knowledge helped justify the European appropriation of land

and resources and the eradication of other kinds of knowing. We now regard this grand narrative with suspicion and try to unsettle those practices.

The third narrative (the speculative one that insists "We can bind all knowledge together and so bind all people who know together with an idea") presumes that the knower and object of knowledge are ultimately identical. In the German tradition, this meant that spirit or mind was seen as progressively realizing itself through all of the sciences. However, this deeply metaphysical view of the world, knowledge, and the knower now seems to most people merely a belief or even a myth. Philosophy abandoned this ideal of holding all knowledge together through a founding metaphysical identity and, by doing so, lost its sovereign role in the university. Without this metaphysical doctrine, the idea of unity could no longer serve as the ultimate goal of our universities, although university leaders might still trot the idea out for rhetorical purposes.

Thus, in 1979, Lyotard had already seen that the traditional university based on a shared grand narrative of established values was disappearing under the force of new information technology. As Lyotard explored the conflicts and limits of different claims to knowing, he was gripped by the pseudohistorical claims of Holocaust deniers. These deniers rigged their determination of what history is to obliterate the Shoah – the destruction of the European Jews and their communities, the burning of their bodies, and the eradication of their records – to deny that any violence had occurred. Genocide, they said, could not be proved.

This was a precursor to the "truth crisis" that led tens of millions of Americans to believe that the 2020 election was stolen. But Lyotard's account of the collapse of the grand narratives is also in some ways a foreshadowing of the crisis in attitudes toward public health that overtook the world during the COVID-19 pandemic.

Loss of unity does not mean that the university is pointless or that diverse local narratives of science can ignore each other. What is missing is an account of how to make sense of what is left when the grand narratives are gone – and how to reorient the education of students to help society work within this lack of unity.

To help make sense of the creative task associated with navigating disunity, I advance the idea of discord: the idea that multiple and conflicting ways of justifying knowledge can inhabit a common space while remaining in disagreement.

That idea of discord will also help us find our way in a network of social practices and forces. When we no longer rage against (or mourn for) the disappearance of grand narratives that depend on the ideas of unity and universality, we can discern a new task: exploring the limits of each science not in terms of its objects but in terms of its method and ways of marking off its own range. Ultimately, the challenge is to explore and discern new paths from one body of knowledge to another without depending on a universal claim. The university is not simply a broken Humpty Dumpty but rather a series of profound gaps that reflect limited, if locally legitimated, interests.

THE IDEA OF DISCORD. The idea that multiple and conflicting ways of justifying knowledge can inhabit a common space. In a university, conflicts between faculties and fields of study, in all their plurality, can be sustained in dynamic tension.

Lyotard defined *terror* as the act of silencing, expelling, or excluding speakers bearing evidence of other interests or other kinds of knowledge. I wish culture wars, the battle over the term *woke,* and the upsurge of hatred and censorship on campuses were novelties – but they are perennial modes of terror. Lyotard articulated, as a fundamental principle, the negative goal: whatever rules, practices, and methods we follow, we should not resort to terror and silencing one another.

In his major work, *The Differend,* Lyotard explored how a damage is actionable in court. One can bring a complaint for a harm done by another to a tribunal, a place to make good a claim to know something that happened.[5] But a differend occurs when there's no court, no tribunal, before which one can bring a complaint for some harm done. This is a wrong: a damage accompanied by the loss of the means to prove the damage. The victims of a genocide lack evidence and a court, so we hope the creation of new international courts and procedures might counter genocide's terror. Lyotard also offered the example of the Martinican, who can bring a complaint against any infringement on her rights as a French citizen but encounters a differend when she tries to bring a case against France for making her a French citizen. Over forty years ago, Lyotard was provoked to explore the limitations of knowledge in the contexts of genocide and colonialism (illustrating just how little progress we've seen).

But Lyotard also articulated the task that can constitute the university. The task of the philosopher is to bear witness to differends, to the places where we cannot yet find the words for a wrong, where it is not yet demonstrable or, we might say, not yet knowable. Here, Lyotard identifies a decisive difference between the theory of language he was developing and economic systems.[6] Indeed, near the end of his book, he criticizes capitalism, communism, and Marxism. While the idea of unity arose from a thirst for a universal humanity, a universal subject, a political form called the state – the subject in practice looked like a white European male, and the state veered toward a total state. In the process, the differend would be betrayed, and a wrong that could not yet present itself would be silenced.

For Lyotard, the sense that capitalism was silencing the voices of the wronged was most significant. It is certainly possible to criticize the university from the left: neoliberalism has been infiltrating and instrumentalizing the university, reducing its value to efficiency in the service of the knowledge economy. This criticism is developed by Lyotard, but he proposes a different analysis and response, one that recognizes multiple wrongs and modes of suffering with gaps that no speculative unity can recoup. What is now called intersectionality is, in Lyotard's thought, recognition that there are many forms of wrong that intersect and compound suffering. A ruling economic genre silences many kinds of wrongs, but there's no unity of the wronged. Claims based on race, indigeneity, class, gender, religion, sexuality, language, history, and culture are each dismissed by the court of efficiency, which requires that knowledge be justified only in the service of economic gain. The university, then, could be the place where intersecting discourses are given voice, where unheard and seemingly impossible sufferings enter into knowledge.

I believe a key task for the university is learning how to recognize these differends. It must explore how to hear the pleas of the harmed. The idea of discord calls on us to preserve disagreement, to recognize that the different practices of knowledge do not need to combine into a deeper agreement. In this context, the idea of inquiry leads us to seek out what is invisible in our own practice of knowing so we can respond.

Lyotard focused on the future of research and claimed we already recognized that different sciences, including the humanities, have various practices. We have to make visible the various ways that current knowledge is incomplete. The loss of universality is not a collapse into nihilism or relativism. The idea of unity presupposes only two choices: a common unity or some sort of anarchy or nihilism. By contrast, the idea of discord can dignify the university's task: to bear witness to the lack of a system to create space for harder disagreements. The idea of discord depends on variety and disagreement among the sciences. It requires research into things unknown, not simply addressing a challenge or discovering a critical gap, but also the work of discerning new rules and new practices or new modes of knowing.

This is consonant with Hermann Cohen's description of research and the creation of possibilities. The university, then, would be a place where instability is supported and encouraged with no hope of domesticating it. To support creative instability, the university must guarantee freedom of inquiry and a haven from terror.

When it's in the service of discord, research performs an ethical task. The three key elements of education discussed in Chapter 1 – knowledge, critique, and inquiry – are changing today. Reflection and questioning, which unsettles information, are central because disparate sources and modes of justifying knowledge provoke people to ask, How can I know if this claim is true? If evaluating knowledge and thinking through how we judge local justifications are processes to be studied and learned, then research is doubled. First, it is a process of seeking new knowledge and new readings of the past, including the need to justify the value of the knowledge gained. Second, gaps and inadequacies, exclusions and multiple kinds of knowledge call for an inquiry that reaches across the sciences, sectors, and divisions of knowledge. It means paying attention to what is unheard today and what was suppressed in the past with the academic freedom to safeguard diverse modes of knowing.

I call this the round and round: the university is neither a top-down hierarchy of knowledge nor a smattering of unconnected schools and disciplines, but rather vigorous interactions among schools and disciplines. Inquiry depends not only on critique but also on the circulation of ideas and discord among the research methods. Each field offers a limited justification for its own insights and practice and has a secured place in the institution. The limitations and gaps, the exclusions and fault lines prompt local-local inquiry, attempts to find ways to translate or adjudicate the differends. This round and round is not a global discourse; it is not a universal reason that can sit in judgment over each claim to science, social policy, or interpretative move. It is not a universal history but rather an ongoing search to exceed local exclusions. The goal, while adhering to one's discipline, is to learn how to hear what does not appear reasonable by the standards of my discipline and to refuse to resort to terror tactics. Consensus will not arise, and it's not the goal. But secure debate and discussion can advance knowledge. Academic freedom, then, is more than simply tolerating opinions or schools of thought you don't agree with; it's a call to attend to one another – to listen and recognize the limitations in your own school and between schools.

Returning to education in the university, a.k.a. the students, I ask, How do the tasks associated with the idea of discord engage undergraduates in a research university? What is the role of university education in a world where students are connected digitally? What can we teach that will help them swim in the flood they live in?

To recap: the question is not so much how to access information but how to evaluate, combine, and criticize it. These reflective practices go beyond merely looking something up. When considering what makes a valuable comment on a blog or news feed, the focus shifts. It's not just about what you want to say or tailoring your tone to fit the context – it's about assessing the rules and practices that justify the claims being made. It might even involve challenging or undermining those claims. One might need to study classic texts, analyze a contemporary viral debate, study a page design, or explore a recent advance in biological science – not so much to learn the claims being advanced, but to see how rules and practices inform the claims and create their own field of knowledge and research.

For born-digital students, learning how to do research is more than simply learning how to search online for what other people have written. A research paper is not a blog. Research is more than employing ChatGPT to canvas what's out there and invent what a relevant answer might be. Research is learning how to define a question that is worthwhile and not yet explored. Research is unpredictable. Learning what to consult and by what method provides students with insights that increase their ability to manoeuvre in the nonuniversity world.

However, the second mode of research, the one where students notice gaps and try to bridge them, is the mode that might be a true justification for a university. Yet it is the most difficult to teach. First, graduate education, which is linked to specialization and mastery of one set of rules and practices, might be in tension with the undergraduate's need to discern and navigate the exclusions and blindsides of research. Second, we now live in a world where we're constantly connected; where our "friends" are aware of our experiences, often in real time; where our followers are receiving too much information in short media posts. Our connectedness poses key questions about how intellectual collaboration will work. Will we have time to think? Does higher education take time? Does research take time? Given the new information technology, which gives students access to information in radically transformed ways – in their pocket and within a cloud of social connections – what role can the university play?

In a move you'll likely expect, I look to a historical episode for the answers: the emergence of the printed book in the fifteenth century, a time when reading practices and learning changed and yet the university still survived.

Designs: Two Pages

Humanities scholars not only study historical materials, especially written texts, but they also explore the history of scholarship itself, the history of study, to examine critically how scholars have justified knowing the past. Our current moment, when the challenge is determining how we'll study, read, and write in the new digital formats, is not the only crisis point in the history of study.

To draw out the parallels and differences between our current moment and the fifteenth and sixteenth centuries, I consider two different models of graphic design in scholarship: the commentary page and the humanist page. I claim that a transition in scholarship is evident in the early modern editions of texts created by the humanists of the fifteenth and sixteenth centuries. But the historical record itself is, of course, more complicated. What I identify here is the emergence of a kind of reading and scholarship that is most familiar to us (humanist) and distinguish it from a mode of reading that is less comfortable (commentary). Comparable technological and design changes are underway today. Will we be able to invent, renew, and revise our scholarship and our research universities in their wake?

Of course, the Gutenberg moment – the invention of movable type, when printed books replaced manuscripts copied by hand, leading to much wider access to written works – has been much-considered and perhaps overtheorized for some time. Similarly, the story of humanism, when philologists (people who study the history of languages) were given free rein to edit and recover the best versions of Greek and Roman texts and challenge contemporary lenses on history, is a much-celebrated story that has also been re-evaluated by critics. What was once seen as the heroic recovery of classical knowledge has been recast many times. The version that interests me focuses on how this shift in reading practices democratized (even commercialized) the book, yes, but also transformed the authority of scholars and the way they read.

The shift in how we "know" was captured or rather generated by the new printed page, a design innovation linked to the printing press and critical textual scholarship.

But let's begin with a "traditional" page, one with commentaries and notes. Illustration 2 is a printed version of the *Babylonian Talmud* from 1576.

The text is a commentary or Gemara from the fifth century CE on a third-century text, the Mishnah. The page has many text blocks. The central text is the Gemara, and the surrounding columns are other commentaries. Indeed, some are hypercommentaries. Who can read such a text? It takes much schooling. Each page bears a wealth of diverse knowledge – neither subordinated nor narratable. Indeed, the page presupposes a library of other books as well as a school. Even in a print economy, this text was not distributed to a mass reading public. It is not hard to see why.

A parallel Christian commentary tradition is evident in Illustration 3, the iconic *Glossa ordinaria*, which gives top billing to Nicholas of Lyra in the print edition of 1498.

2 *Babylonian Talmud,* 1576

Glossa ordinaria is a compendium of Christian commentators on the Bible. Here, too, we see a wide range of text blocks: translations, commentaries, glosses, moral teachings, and so forth. Here, too, are a series of interlinear glosses and marginal cross-references. The printed editions began in the fifteenth century, but the original editions go back to the twelfth century, and the *Glossa* came into its own in the fourteenth century. There is comparative translation from Greek at work here, but the texts are in Latin. We see more than a few echoes of manuscript pages and formats, and just like Talmudic pages printed hundreds of years later, the pages have been enhanced in interesting ways by movable type.

Commentary texts from China and other traditions abound in different periods. I'm not telling a strictly linear story here. The point is that scholars often prefer to study a page that locates the text under consideration in a sea of commentary, notes, glosses, translations, and so forth. This is a type of page, a page for study and scholarship. What interests me

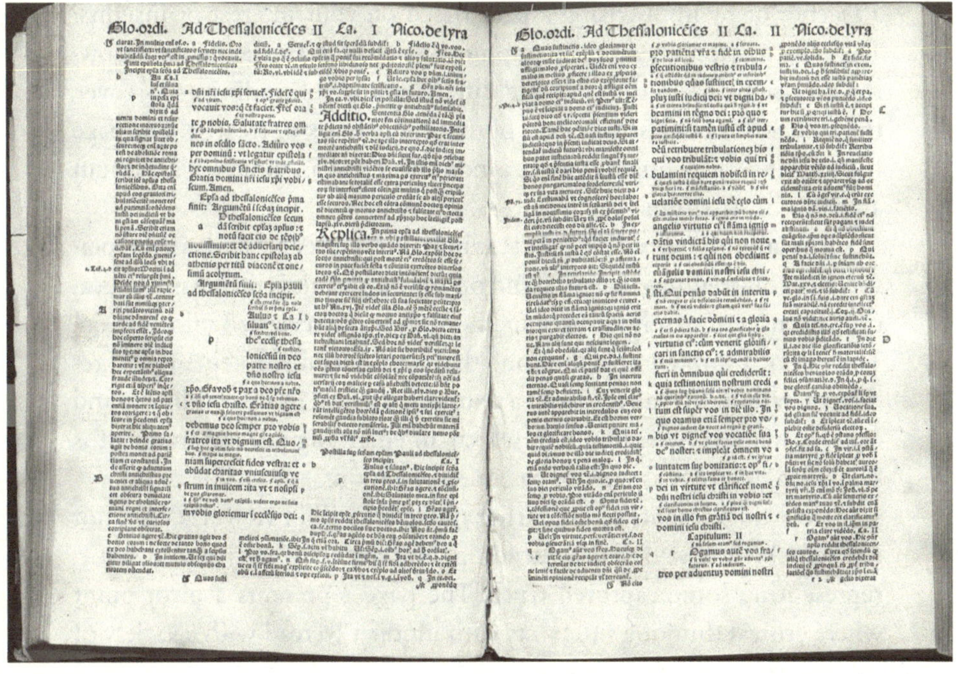

3 *Glossa ordinaria,* 1498

is the similarities between the multiple text blocks and the vitality of the commentary on the same page. But manuscripts did this too. In other words, the technology did not simply determine the design of the page.

Consider the kind of learning and thinking that occurs in studying such a text. Past readers hold authority over the contemporary reader. The scholar doesn't approach the original text (itself often a narrative or an account of past events) in isolation from other readings. In the *Glossa,* the separate text blocks demand an ongoing interaction with past readers. The scholar does not simply recite the "primary" text but rather rereads the commentaries – in all their complexity. Some are commentaries on other commentaries; some are cross-references; some are directed to specific perspectives.

Does reading require you to engage with all the text on the page? Or is reading the process of finding a visual path to draw together some portion of the information displayed, either by following a path set by a teacher or by improvising a path based on your interest or insights? The information, in short, is graphically presented to facilitate following diverse paths on the page and different kinds of readings. Moreover, the core text is but a small piece of the whole book or treatise. The page has a nonnarrative quality – time is nonlinear and, in some ways, without an efficient structure.

Importantly, rereading past readings offers leverage and critical perspectives on readings that do stand on the page. This is university education, in contrast to schooling, which simply transfers tested information. This is not a unified field, but one that harbours disagreement and reinterpretation. To read is to join a tradition marked by discontinuity and change, marked by readings in which an emerging present moment is bound to different aspects of past interpretations.

The achievements of the earlier phase are still in view; they are not replaced by a new definitive reading. Nor are they eternal and static, representing some captured truth. The page represents a pivot point where critical thinking intersects with inquiry. To read with a variety of past interpreters is to seek a new reading.

The word *invention* has a rich history in reading and rhetoric. Prior to the invention of what we would recognize as modern machines and processes, *invention* often meant "a quest for new interpretations." The idea of inquiry requires an unsettling of knowledge; hence, a small bit of canonical text is subjected to iterations of questioning and recontextualizing, and the work of reading aims to produce another comment, a new reading of the earlier multiple readings or even a new reading of the source text. We see on the page waves of invention and criticism. Different views from different times and places are placed against one another, and the readers learn to think with historical documents in a way that challenges the claims of a settled story or normalized interpretation in our own time, opening up a configured place for inquiry.

As for the readers, there's a sociality on the page often repeated in the classroom or study house. Just as the text is constructed to be intertextual, so the reading practice is interpersonal. Some in the room may be teachers and authorities; others may be novices, ignorant not only of the content but also of the practice of navigating the texts. Some rooms may be devoted to reading among equals, to long-term partners or circles

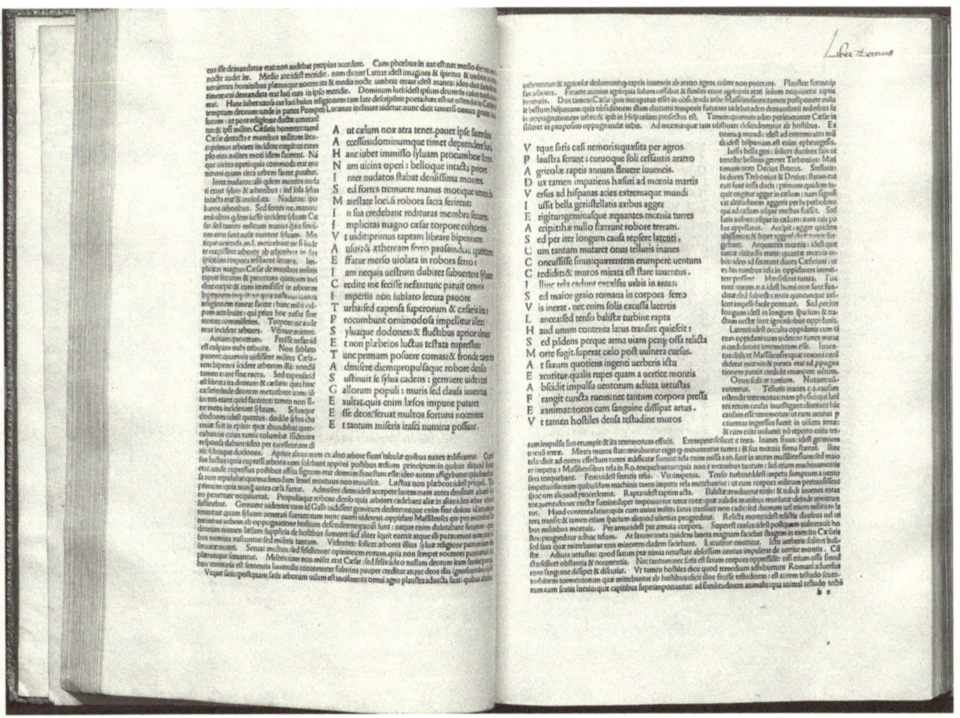

4 Lucan, *Pharsalia,* 1486

who are familiar with one another and with different commentators and traditions. This kind of study takes a long time. In a Talmud class, one page might take a week, and the class will arrive at multiple truths and solutions. In this social reading, exchanges among the readers illuminate exchanges on the page. There is inquiry. This is a specific kind (or perhaps a root) of humanities research.

I've begun with sacred scriptures, but we need to ask a question that goes to the heart of the humanists and the humanities (their descendants). Is there a difference between holy texts and profane ones? Is there a boundary, in the West for instance, between scriptures and classics and how they are printed and studied?

Illustration 4 is a page from Lucan's *Pharsalia,* a first-century epic history printed in 1486, similarly composed of multiple blocks of commentaries.

LVC.

S anguine, & hoſtilem defectis robore membris
I nſiluit ſolo nociturus pondere puppim.
S trage uirum cumulata ratis, multoq; cruore
P lena, per obliquum crebros latus accipit ictus,
A t poſtquam ruptis pelagus compagibus hauſit,
A d ſummos repleta foros deſcendit in undas,
V icinum inuoluens contorto uertice pontum.
A equora diſcedunt merſa diducta carina,
I nq; locum puppis cecidit mare, multaq; ponto
P raebuit illa dies uarii miracula fati.
F errea dum puppis rapidos manus inſerit uncos,
A ffixit Lycidam. merſus foret ille profundo,
S ed prohibent ſocii, ſuſpenſaq; crura retentant,
S cinditur auulſus, nec ſicut uulnere ſanguis
E micuit lentus, ruptis cadit undique uenis,
D iſcurſusq; animae diuerſa in membra meantis
I nterceptus aquis. nullius uita perempti
E ſt tanta dimiſſa uia. pars ultima trunci
T radidit in letum uacuos uitalibus artus.
A t tumidus qua pulmo iacet, qua uiſcera feruent,
H aeſerunt ibi fata diu, luctataq; multum
H ac cum parte uiri uix omnia membra tulerunt,
D um nimium pugnax unius turba carinae
I ncumbit prono lateri, uacuamq; relinquit,
Q ua caret hoſte, ratem, congeſto pondere puppis
V erſa caua texit pelagus, nautasq; carina,
B rachia nec licuit uaſto iactare profundo,
S ed clauſo periere mari. tunc unica diri
C onſpecta eſt leti facies. cum forte natantem
D iuerſae roſtris iuuenem fixere carinae,

LIB.III.

D iſceſſit medium tam uaſtos pectus ad ictus,
N ec prohibere ualent obtritis oſſibus artus,
Q uo minus aera ſonent, eliſo uentre per ora
E iectat ſaniem permixtus uiſcere ſanguis.
P oſtquam inhibēt remis puppes, ac roſtra recedūt,
D eiectum in pelagus perfoſſo pectore corpus
V ulneribus tranſmiſit aquas. pars maxima turbae
N aufragae iactatis morti obluctata lacertis,
P uppis ad auxilium ſociae concurrit at illi
R obora cum uetitis prenſarent altius ulnis,
N utaretq; ratis populo peritura recepto,
I mpia turba ſuper medios ferit enſe lacertos
B rachia linquentes graia pendentia puppe,
A manibus cecidere ſuis, non amplius undae
S uſtinuere graues in ſummo gurgite truncos.
I amq; omni fuſis nudato milite telis,
I nuenit arma furor, remum contorſit in hoſtem
A lter, at hi totum ualidis apluſtre lacertis,
A uulſasq; rotant excuſſo remige ſedes,
I n pugnam fregere rates. ſidentia peſſum
C orpora caeſa tenent, ſpoliantq; cadauera ferro.
M ulti inopes teli, iaculum letale reuulſum
V ulneribus traxere ſuis, & uiſcera leua
O ppreſſere manu ualidos dum praebeat ictus
S anguis, & hoſtilem cum torſerit exeat haſtam.
N ulla tamen plures hoc edidit aequore clades,
Q uam pelago diuerſa lues, nam pinguibus ignis
A ffixus taedis, & tecto ſulfure uiuax
S pargitur, ac faciles praebere alimenta carinae
N unc pice, nunc liquida rapuere incendia caera

5 Lucan's *Pharsalia,* designed and printed by Aldus Manutius, 1502

The tradition of scholarly commentaries extended to works of literature, histories, scientific books, and so forth. Learning is learning. And here, as in with the holy texts, little of the original text is on the page compared with the commentary. Again, we see a tendency to accumulate layers of tradition.

Gutenberg's printing press often plays the hero in the story of the emergence of modernity. But I wish to focus our attention on the people who set texts into print: the printers-compositors. These great printers were also designers and editors. These two tasks – page design and editing – required significant negotiation with past readings and with the task of reading itself.

Consider Aldus Manutius, one of the heroes of the humanist moment. Illustration 5 is a page from his 1502 edition of Lucan's *Pharsalia* (Illustration 4). For current book lovers, Manutius is a font designer extraordinaire (the creator of Aldine fonts). He was also a printer, an editor, and in some profound way one who taught us to read the way we do.

What do we see? A single text block, uniform in shape, uncluttered by commentaries, by marginalia, by other texts, and certainly by other fonts.

A single-language text to be read by a single reader. We recognize this as the type of book we read now. It is printed to be read on its own – with no explicit intertext, no links to other passages, no recourse to the thinking of previous readers.

The humanists were an editorial movement. Using philological skill and knowledge, printers struggled to determine the original text. They compared variants, explored grammar, and developed lexica. The "pure" humanist text was the result of extensive editing and correcting – and the variants (at least in many editions) were hidden. The reader was delivered a product shorn of the mess of corrupt copying and misguided accreted commentaries, a text free of apparatus and free of debate. Just the "true" text of a classic. This was a new kind of scholarship with a new reader. Its very clarity and simplicity hid the intricacy of the humanists' scholarly engagement.

If the commentary page represents a sea of thinkers and writers, a world of diverse minds engaged with a limited set of words, then the humanist page represents the solitary author. The reader, too, is solitary. An individual arises here who is not linked to or called by a series of past readers, nor is this reader necessarily in conversation with contemporary readers. Printing made book production much less expensive. The costs could be borne by the reader, who did not need a school in which to read. This page can be freely read without joining a tradition or taking a side in an ongoing argument. The reader can engage with the original text.

Time changes too. The text is now contemporary with the reader. If the reader can safely ignore previous readers, then the reader can read in the same time or era of the text's printing, in the time of its author. The text's authority is direct and unmediated, making time stand still. The text has become information; it represents knowledge and settled matters. But my own licence – indeed, my own authority as a reader – is undiluted by the task of sorting and positioning my thinking in relation to multiple texts. The veils and media of interpretation are discarded. I learn to read the original. Such a text does not require a library; it does not require a circle or a classroom. The reader can be solitary, learning to think as an individual with an individual author. This kind of page is, I suggest, the design from which the modern subject arises.

Finally, this is a page that can be read quickly. Some words might be difficult, but the work does not drive you around the page. The eye moves in a linear, easy manner through the text to the next page. It takes some time to read, but the ease of motion creates a new velocity and a transparency of information. The effort of reading is reduced. The text seems to immediately answer the questions posed; indeed, it welcomes the reader into a solitary world.

Would novels exist without this page? When we read a novel, our reading happens in an ever-expanding present bound to its determined goal: reaching the end of the book. Unlike the novel, the commentary page offers no predictable ending; indeed, no closure is possible. How do we make sense of the tension between sudden shifts of voice and the puzzle-like skills required to read the commentary page?

Scholarship, then, moved from being a scholastic effort that occurs in a scholarly language on a complex page within a community of scholars to a tool with one simple goal: legibility. The humanist page is the accessible product of much scholarship. When we enter the world of translation, we see the tension between scholars and the common people brought into focus. If the text of the Bible can save its listeners and readers, then it must speak to them in their own language. This era is a new stage when the Bible and books are written in the vernacular for a wider public. They are books meant to be read with an intimacy of address as though you were directly addressed by the author. The theologian's work has been rendered merely academic.

The temporality of the humanist page carried forward into biblical editions and, indeed, translations. The Reformation's great insight was that the reader should be placed in biblical time; the text speaks to you, here and now. Salvation is not just a past event; it is witnessed in the present and for the future. To make this immediacy possible, the historical layers of interpretation and the web of prior readings are stripped away. Missteps – and even correct interpretations– are hidden, allowing the reader to encounter the divine word directly on the page. Much depends on the translator, editor, and printer, but the reader sees only the text before them and thus engages with God's word directly. This openness makes the word accessible to every individual, bypassing the traditional settings of study circles, classrooms, or religious institutions. However, this radical accessibility also sparked debates about control and the authority of translations.

These two different kinds of pages – the commentary page and the humanist page – allow us to see how reading and writing are incarnate: they live in the materiality of the things we study. The act of reading in these two textual environments is remarkably different. Reading the humanist page occurs in a kind of solitary authority – other voices are quelled, and each reader has a chance to develop her own thoughts, to think for herself. Reading the commentary page, the reader discerns that her reading is incomplete. No commentator or editor is the final word on a text. No text is ever fully present – or, rather, the present is overflowing, awaiting more readers. Reading is social, and thinking is learning to respond to other people's questions; in some important way, the text remains open to future readers.

This openness, I would also suggest, can be linked to the idea of multiplication. Ironically, an increase in the number of copies of books (and, hence, of readers) led to a practice of reading that was less social, a type of thinking that could be more private. The independence of reading a private copy helped create a self responsible only for itself.

By contrast, having a multiplicity of texts and readers in a shared space offers a rich model for multiplied inquiry. We write commentary not to close the discussion but to re-engage with the past text to hold it open for future readers, who are responsible for oncoming generations of readers.

The opposition I've drawn might be unstable, but this moment we call "early modern" provided a key innovation. Recovering and publicizing the original texts was not simply noble – it was revolutionary. Some texts appeared in classical languages, others in the vernacular. Some were sacred, some were profane. The fruits were split between scholars and the emerging reading public. *Split* is too polite a word for the effect. Books were burned, and many people were put to death and fled into exile – and, of course, these conflicts resulted in the overthrow of churches, states, and even universities.

If I've simplified both the history of page design and the emergence of modernity, the goal has been to accentuate how a change in reading and writing was bound up with a change in the authority of readers (and writers). Universities were, indeed, the battlefields, and the Reformation produced many martyrs among the ranks of scholars. (A colleague from the Faculty of Divinity at Cambridge observed that for well over a century no professor died in his bed!)

One could tell another, more familiar, story: the story of the modern university as a struggle to address the revolution of reading, as the rise of modern science, as the emergence of thought unbound to generations of commentators. In each case, the university played a role in the struggle to control who has access to information, teaching not only how to master but also how to question and advance it. All that is at the core of our universities. But for my purposes, we need only have a sense of the crisis linked to this humanist page and the university to contend with the challenge we're facing today.

How Will We Read and Write?

I'd like to conclude this chapter with the claim that our current change in information technology requires a similar transformation in how scholars read and write.

It's clear to me that while students are out in front, traditions have much to offer.

When AI shifted from being something imagined as futural to something confronting universities – and all of society – concern about the place of essay writing in the humanities gained a sharper edge. To take a step back from the pressing moment, I explore older humanities practices that are valuable to the new environment. The humanities have the distinctive asset of a longer tradition: an awareness of the capacity to change and to reconfigure past and present practices.

When I began directing and planning the Jackman Humanities Institute, several advisers encouraged me to look into the digital humanities. I could write a whole chapter about our various attempts, mostly failed, to find a way to support digital humanities at the University of Toronto, which is ironic, given the University of Toronto was a pioneer in the field over thirty years ago. Some disciplines were resistant to changing their methods along with new technology; others were trail-blazing.

In any case, we commissioned a census of research professors and their projects and discovered seventy professors were funded to do digital humanities. Scholars were engaged in diverse projects: assembling databases of archaeological findings, artworks, or historical languages; creating dictionaries; mapping communications or scholarship networks; developing visualizations and augmented reality; and hosting digital co-laboratories to engage students and other universities in explorations of medieval text culture or contemporary issues in Indigenous studies. Many of our most creative scholars were engaging with the new technology to pursue new research.

In the wake of the census, we created our second research community: the Digital Humanities Network. It grew rapidly to more than 220 members, including 150 research professors engaged in over one hundred projects. The Jackman Humanities Institute didn't fund or coordinate this sprawling set of activities and research; we hosted a network through workshops, conferences, and pilot fellowships. We saw that graduate students and sometimes undergraduates were taking the lead on these activities, and links with computer science and other sciences led the institute beyond the humanities.

One project (or, rather, a preproposal or call for a proof of concept by a group of readers) in which I was involved illustrated new thinking about how long-standing practices in the humanities might preview the future of reading and writing.

Scriptural Reasoning is a community of scholars that has been meeting for over twenty-five years, primarily at Cambridge University and the University of Virginia but also with key participation at the University of Toronto.[7] Readers from the Christian, Islamic, and Jewish religious traditions meet in small groups and read parallel texts from the three traditions, paying careful attention to the complex meanings in each tradition. As scholars, we aren't seeking common ground or trying to convert one another; we are exploring other ways of reading and deepening our understanding of our own traditions. This kind of study relates to the idea of discord: the goal is not to find a deeper unity but to seek new paths to bridge gaps between traditions.

Some time ago, in conversations with some software developers, a few of us imagined an online form for this activity. We were joining in a quest for what I called "the Holy Grail of digital humanities": a flexible online commentary platform. The obstacles were numerous: multiple languages, alphabets, canonical texts, and, of course, willing participants. (In the intervening years, new platforms for commentary have emerged, for instance, Perusall. But the goal of creating an adequate platform still animates various digital humanities projects.) In the process of imagining an online model – a model we did not succeed in building – we recognized three distinct practices: (1) collecting, (2) writing commentary, and (3) editing. The first would be the practices of selecting what belongs in the library; the second would be practices of responding to specific texts or published matters; and the third would be sorting, and reducing, and consolidating the creative commentary work, in order to publish new texts.

First, we would need to create a common library of the editions we wanted to cite and comment on, and we needed to choose which translations we would use. The library would need to include the traditional commentaries, the lexica, concordances, and some scholarly materials (old and new). The initial question was not how to digitize materials but what should be collected. (Digitization would require clear protocols for tagging to allow ready access, searching, and so on.)

Second, we wanted a safe, semiprivate (or is it "small public"?) space for registering our comments and responding to one another's comments. In real time, and over time, we wanted a wiki-like conversation, or something of the sort, where our group and maybe other parallel groups could read together and write our thoughts, large and small. Comments might be on a specific word and its history, a larger theme (for example, diverse written versions of laws or stories), or our own commenting interactions.

Third, at regular intervals, we wanted a smaller group of scholars to edit the commentaries to present their fruit to a wider public. That fruit might be a single dramatic new insight, a debate, a new reading, or a program of questions that emerged from the comments. This eventual, distilled publication would create space for a freer, more expansive, and experimental exchange among the group of commentators. The knowledge that later editors would refine the work would remove the pressure of finality, allowing discussions in this earlier stage to unfold more openly.

As I indicated, there are many scholars, labs, and groups working on developing commentary platforms. My point is that these three practices have been long-standing in the humanities. They go back to the humanists of the early modern era and beyond. They can, however, be revitalized in new digital environments, and humanities scholars are the ones most likely to make direct contributions to deepening the reading and writing of the future. Whereas the idea of unity would have us seek out a shared foundation or even methodology for these explorations, the idea of discord respects a plurality of traditions and languages. Indeed, discord is a positive resource for this new kind of platform.

In a truly fascinating way, university libraries are not only reacting to changes in reading but are leading the way. Librarians model and support old and new practices. Libraries are not simply collections but also sites for discussions and places that assist and guide collaborative research.

Thus, in terms of collecting or assembling the library, research in the future will need to sift through and privilege better sources. Google Books, for instance, is an ever-improving hodgepodge of virtual books. To reflect critically, to explore the limits of existing information, or to seek new knowledge, a person would need to learn how to assemble a relevant data set. In the humanities, for instance, there can be different critical editions (thank you, humanists) of a given text. Scholar can assess which are best and base their readings on the superior editions.

But as much as we need to assemble the best library, we also need to learn how to evaluate the vast array of information available online. Beyond searching using Google or Google Scholar or DuckDuckGo, we need to judge what should be included. An educated person can learn how to sort, prioritize, and exclude from the flood of information available to determine which of the old canonical texts and dictionaries are best and which sources for researching contemporary culture are dependable.

Commenting on texts is the ancestor of blogging. The ability to repost, offer my views, and criticize what others have said about another person's post is now unrestricted. But what makes a good comment? Is the citation index (the number of times others cite something) the measure of a good comment? Perhaps obscurity or minimal citation is a mark of wisdom, of the rarer insight. While many great commentators in the past were individuals, they were rarely solitary. They shared their comments with one another, and their readings were sometimes preserved. Those early commentary pages are the equivalent of having multiple windows open in a browser. Reading is finding a way through these sources, and commenting is adding our own voices.

Finally, while tools like wiki editors, metablogs, and emerging AI tools help consolidate the vast array of communications on the web, the practice of redaction remains uniquely valuable. Selecting the best materials from our group's collective efforts – deciding what to share to advance research and knowledge – requires distinctive skills. While AI can use algorithms to sort and digest and bots can proliferate provocative comments, the kinds of thinking that advance inquiry descend naturally from humanistic research. Humanities scholars serve as editors of journals, book series, and edited works, and most review other people's work for publication – our disciplines cultivate judgment on what is worth sharing. Can we teach this in the new context so that people can learn not only from ready experience but also from reflective and thoughtful engagement with knowledge? Can we revise the work of humanities scholars to educate students on better practices for thinking as they navigate the online world?

The task of the university in our digitally mediated world is more vast than collecting, commenting, and editing, and there are many other ways to conduct data analysis or learn how to navigate information online. But reading and writing are now unremitting. In earlier generations, small groups of people wrote letters, constantly. This is, in fact, a topic of study among humanities scholars. In our time, *everyone* is constantly reading and writing – through email, Facebook, TikTok, X, Instagram, and so on. We are caught up in a semiotic exchange. Media literacy *is* a learning outcome in many schools. Universities have a unique responsibility and capacity for teaching the kinds of thinking that will deepen and transform widely accessible information, limit terror, and find new ways to discern the differends.

One of the new tasks for the humanities, specifically, is to revise and recast our traditions of scholarship for this new context. If you'll forgive the pun, we should take a page from the humanists. We need to design new protocols to engage our students' insatiable desire to read and write in these new environments so they will learn how to reflect and search for new knowledge. The challenge is speed. The commentary page is much slower to read than the humanist page. The current reading pace is faster still – even though the time it takes a person to read a whole text might be quite long because they're constantly jumping to other windows, following chains of connection away from the original text.

The kind of reading and thinking and writing that scholars pursue takes time. Perhaps, in part, what university education needs to do is slow reading and writing down. We now have rapid access to sources, which means we have more time for thinking and questioning. But having more time for reflection, rereading, revising, and rewriting is in tension with current views on efficiency and productivity. Going slowly might yield greater long-term benefits. Fostering habits of reflection, exploration, and discernment that lead to more valuable comments – this is a task for the university. The challenge of designing new ways to navigate the digital environment to serve inquiry is a task for the humanities.

4

Thinking Like a Professional and Responding to Society's Questions

In the spring of 2020, at the very moment when COVID-19 was breaking out, I had a chance to teach an undergraduate course titled "Ethical Enterprise and Critical Reflection." The course was typically about entrepreneurship, innovation, and business ethics. It probably won't surprise you, but it surprised the students, that I focused the course on how these students hoped to change the world. I engaged them in thinking about research.

They were responsible for doing limited research, presenting their questions or results, and commenting on one another's research. Much of the course was focused on professional schools and how a professional education might help prepare people to innovate and become agents of change. I invited professors from various fields and schools (physics, engineering, finance, law, medicine, sustainability, pharmacy) to address the students. Frankly, despite well-grounded assumptions that the professions are conservative and preserve power and status, the academic leaders were inspiring. Arts and science undergraduates gained exposure to the "think like a lawyer or engineer or doctor" of the professional schools and saw up close how their programs differed from professional degrees.

More interesting, many students explored how certain professional schools were innovating and changing. The schools were connecting their students to communities and practitioners and transforming their practice of research. Because these undergraduates had no loyalty to any profession and had not yet been professionalized, they sought out creative spaces where inquiry flourished in the professional schools, which caused them to reflect on the role that learning the logic of inquiry had played in their education in the humanities and social sciences. Studying different professions offered students a merry-go-round understanding of different ways to create a better future, and their experiences offered me a way to reflect on what I call the "round and round" of the university.

If teaching settled information is not the primary goal of university education, then what is? What often comes to mind is getting students job-ready – teaching the skills that the job market requires so students can make a living. But students are thinking about changing the world, not just getting ahead. Some are eager to engage with climate change; others want to design new kinds of information technology; others want to advocate for their own or other oppressed or underrepresented groups; and still others want to help cure cancer. Advocates for the liberal arts and sciences often hesitate or, more bluntly, reject calls for education to make students job-ready. They are also suspicious of societal organizations or agencies directing research. But, as I've outlined in Chapter 2, research can meet society's rapidly changing needs.

The picture gets much more complicated if we add professional schools into these debates. Almost 30 percent of university students are studying to complete a professional degree in medicine, law, social work, engineering, nursing, pharmacy, education, business, music, and so on. They may be studying for professional master's degrees – doctor of medicine (MD), master of social work (MSW), master of business administration (MBA), master of nursing (MN), master of education (MEd), master of information (MI), master of laws (LLM), master of music (MMus), and so on. Some are pursuing a second degree, following a bachelor of arts or science. But some are first-entry degrees, the first degree a student earns. In some countries, medicine and law are always first-entry degrees. Isn't a student with a professional degree job-ready?

Vocational training in a polytechnic or what in Canada we often call "colleges" is the paradigm for job-ready education. Someone training to be an electrician, game designer, or baker learns the information and skills required and, ideally, is connected with an apprenticeship or internship so they can pursue their career and earn a living at the program's end.

Education for a trade or craft is an important path – part of the four kinds of learning in postsecondary education I identified in Chapter 1: (1) learning how to do research, (2) engaging in critical reflection that unsettles knowledge, (3) learning settled knowledge and information, and (4) practice (through an internship, co-op, practicum, or apprenticeship). Many jobs, especially in the trades and technical fields, require advanced training and much knowledge (3 and 4). It would be a mistake to neglect these important sectors of our society just because they do not require critique and inquiry, the two main parts of university education we tracked in the previous chapters (or at least not in the same extended form).

But education for a profession is not the same as education in a trade, and it is not simply a question of salary, class, or status. What is professional education beyond the combination of acquiring knowledge (3) and a practicum (4)? In most discussions that address the purpose of a university education, the professional faculties are simply ignored.

One of the clearest signs that we need new ideas for better university leadership is this: professional schools such as medicine, engineering, and business are used to justify the university. Professional schools attract large investments (as do some other fields), and they yield high-impact discoveries and inventions that change our world. The knowledge discovered in these areas of the university is applied, translated, and mobilized in society. But the research questions come from society, from outside the university, most often in relation to specific clients – people suffering with problems because of limits in our existing knowledge.

Arts and sciences researchers are often suspicious of this emphasis on the social benefits, or impact, of research. They believe the freedom of inquiry is under threat. Surely, they argue, we don't want corporations, the military, or social movements determining the scope and point of our research. To insist on "impact" at the outset betrays science and the independence of university research. They can imagine someone doing research at a corporation or for some other institution having a strictly defined task, but the university needs to be a place of freedom.

This tension between research that responds to social needs (undertaken in professional schools) and research that is more radically free (in the arts and sciences) is a second kind of discord, one inherited from the history of universities and one that engages directly with the question of academic freedom.

In professional schools, we see a specific place for society's questions in their research agendas and teaching. That is, professional schools offer a university education that emphasizes the university's and the student's responsibility to focus on questions that arise not from the disciplines but from real people. The professional school model yields new insights into the kind of thinking a research university can teach its students.

What Is Education in a Profession?

To qualify to practice a profession requires years of higher education. Sometimes the professions have insisted that the combination of knowledge and apprenticeship is all that is needed – that the university is *not* the proper place to learn. Critics have suggested that some professional schools do not belong inside the university. Sometimes, the universities have agreed. Chiropractic is an easy example of a contested case for a university education. But even law has chosen, at times, to stay clear of the university. Given the model of apprenticeship outside the university, what do the professions expect their students to learn in the university? What is the university's distinctive contribution that warrants linking the professional schools to the university? Again, one could make arguments based on financial edge, real estate, or status: the professions want to share the university's social benefits. But our concern is, what is the distinctive intellectual contribution of the university, particularly the research university?

In most professional programs, university courses do not offer practical experience. After a law degree, students article or study before attempting the bar exam; in medicine, students go on to internships or residencies. In many professions, university courses are not in themselves adequate demonstration of mastery of the requisite knowledge. For example, in accounting, students must study for the chartered professional accountant exam.

In the university degree program, students do more than simply acquire knowledge or complete their practical training. Sometimes, professional education is characterized as "learning how to think like a P." Courses in some programs bear "Think Like a Doctor" titles, as do reports, popular columns, and books. While "thinking like an P" means different things depending on the profession, in all cases, *thinking like* is not the same as *knowing*.

In these professions, a specific kind of thinking is linked to making professional judgments. Professions often address cases. Professional education involves case studies that teach a kind of thinking that tests settled knowledge by examining how it fits specific cases. This approach is similar to the critical reflection Schleiermacher saw as the task of the university, although it's not quite the same. In Schleiermacher's time, the undergraduate degree was linked to the civil service, which is close to contemporary professional education. In his model, most undergraduate students did not go on to become researchers, nor did they remain in the university as professors.

No matter how much information is required to become a professional, a university education fosters a kind of thinking and reflection that goes beyond simply acquiring settled knowledge. Moreover, each profession requires a distinctive way of thinking, requiring not just expertise but also a deep engagement with its unique intellectual approach.

The expansion of public access to information (traditionally restricted to professionals) has created groups of people who are over-informed but lack the thinking skills that characterize the professional – people who do not know how to sort and judge information about legal or medical matters, people who could not be trusted to build highway bridges or develop new information technology. During a heated debate, when someone announces they have done research online, you have to wonder whether there has been a deficient amount of "thinking like a P." Accessing information is not the same as thinking and reflection; it does not mean one has grasped how to learn from new cases.

So professional higher education does include questioning and reflecting critically on settled matters. But does it include research? Does thinking like a doctor or engineer employ the logic of inquiry? Professors in professional schools are researchers, so there's always some place for engaging with research within those schools. But is research taught in a professional school simply to recruit a few PhD students from among the lawyers, nurses, doctors, engineers, teachers, and social workers? Is the goal of the research simply to replicate professors? If so, the research would concern only a few PhD students (as discussed in Chapter 2). It would not be a part of the professional students' education.

If the goal of university education is to have students reflect on how we learn so they can unsettle the information we have (an activity that involves navigating a flood of digital information and opinion), then including research in professional schools still requires a further step. Learning research as part of learning how to think like a professional is complicated because the professions vary. It's hard to imagine medicine today without major research activities. But do medical school students and graduates heading off to clinics need to learn how to conduct medical research? Does the now widespread problem-based learning approach in medical schools represent the idea of inquiry (or does it serve the ideas of knowledge and critique)? Conversely, is an intensely research-oriented faculty of medicine fit to teach clinical physicians their profession?

We need, yet again, to consider students who are not going on to a PhD – this time, the professional students. They need to be able to continue learning. Indeed, reflection and questioning of settled matters is a key part of what the university offers them. But what would be the value of learning how to discover new knowledge?

Thinking about the social role of knowledge in the professions can help us look at research from a new angle. A student who enrols for an engineering degree or a medical degree is usually not planning to become a professor of engineering or medicine. But the professions address problems and questions that are valuable to society – how to build a new road, treat a pandemic, create a better policy for the elderly, and so on. To learn a profession is to learn the thinking needed to solve these problems well and safely for society.

Research in the professions, then, aims to enhance the capacity of professionals to help their clients. This is a major reason why the university can cheer and extol the research being undertaken in these fields. It's not really about the professors and their status but about the social benefits of their research. The professional student learns the logic of inquiry in a way that attends to clients and to society and its future needs. The professions practise a rich responsibility beyond the university, even when they're situated in the university.

A clear example is the paradigm emerging for the study of Indigenous law in Canada, represented in particular by the University of Victoria's Faculty of Law. Students are closely engaged in research with Indigenous communities and experts, including extensive on-site, off-campus learning. The program mixes traditional common law courses with courses that teach the specific methods of inquiry needed to discern not only past legal traditions but also questions arising in the Indigenous communities. To be able to think like an Indigenous lawyer means having control over unsettling and challenging legal knowledge, but it also requires the skills of inquiry and (as we'll see) listening and attending to the questions of the communities the future lawyers will serve. Here is an expanding vision not only of who can practise a profession (Indigenous people were banned in Canada from hiring lawyers until 1951, and few Indigenous people were called to the bar before the 1980s) but also of the range of study and place of research in the practice of the professional.

In every area of the university, people are debating what students should be learning about research. It's often argued that only PhD students and professors should be conducting research. In the humanities, for instance, the creative arts are in tension with more established modes of scholarly research: Does a creative artistic project "count" as research? In the social sciences, people are debating activism and its place in scientific research. In engineering, some people say design thinking is what students need to learn but engineering research is something else. In medicine, there's a tension between clinical education and research on medical practice and scientific and pharmacological research. These debates and negotiations reflect the challenge of defining research and its role in student education.

To complicate things, universities often offer the possibility of studying beyond the narrow bounds of a professional school. This might be a professional ethics course, a history course, or even a cognate science. The university's breadth can enhance a professional student's education, and professional societies sometimes encourage this kind of enhancement. Other times, they're suspicious and uninterested. Does a profession benefit from broadening its students' thinking? If so, might students in the arts and sciences also benefit from studying with professional students?

The Ideas of Freedom and Responsibility

Students in professional schools learn how to "think like a P." The professions have societies that regulate professionals, certify who is qualified, and accredit schools to provide educational preparation. Professional societies (not the university) determine what the education for a profession should be. Thus, a university's professional programs are for the most part accredited by professional boards, and graduates require subsequent certification to become professionals. The professional bodies are usually licensed by the government. They are known as colleges, institutes, societies, councils, or associations. Governments, representing society, recognize that professionals, not the civil service, should set the standards for a profession. Governments fund and regulate universities (with respect for some sort of autonomy) and also grant regulatory authority to the professions over themselves.

Other forces are at work in the professions' role in the university. A complex negotiation for the number of student slots takes place between the government, the profession, and the university. Control of access has economic implications and has often led to ethnic and gender biases. The university rarely has unregulated control over the size of the cohorts entering the arts and the sciences let alone the professional schools. Through these mediating bodies, society makes many claims on the university, and, in some important way, these declared needs for higher education are the foundational way that the university serves society.

I call the university's task of responding to societal claims the idea of responsibility.

THE IDEA OF RESPONSIBILITY. The capacity to respond to another person and often to be bound to do so. In the university, there are many kinds of responsibility, but in terms of thinking, it is the responsibility to think in response to a question from another person.

The arts and sciences in general regard mediated control in the professional schools with suspicion. There are no societies or councils that regulate the curriculums of a humanities department, or even a physical science department. Instead, there's a distinctive kind of freedom that is not always captured by the phrase *academic freedom* but allows teaching and research to proceed according to their own rules. In the arts and sciences, undergraduate curriculums, programs, and the scope of inquiry are rarely accountable to an accrediting body. No mediating body speaks on behalf of the educational needs of undergraduates. Only professors have a say in the shape of PhD education. Self-regulation, or autonomy, to use a philosophical word, is the norm. This image of autonomy is clearly linked to the autonomy of the professions.

The conflict over the place of mediating societies in professional schools and arts and sciences is a conflict between the idea of freedom and the idea of responsibility – and this is a conflict that has long helped make universities what they are. Clearly, research seeks truth – reliable insight into the world as it is and trustworthy accounts of how we should live in the future. So, does the university serve truth for its own sake (freedom) or does it serve truth in relation to external powers (responsibility)?

THE IDEA OF FREEDOM. To not be subjected to coercive control and, thus, to choose actions for oneself. In the university, there is a general sense of academic freedom, which sustains the right to state truths that are critical and unpopular. Here, it is the freedom to pursue research without constraint or censorship.

In Chapter 3, I introduced the idea of discord, and I'm afraid the history of the university offers more than a few examples of discord. Control and authority over the university have usually been in question. Scholars in critical university studies tend to focus on the neoliberal assault on freedom and emancipation (grand narratives that are no longer binding, according to Lyotard). But "interference" with academic freedom has a much longer history, and one of the most insightful accounts of discord is found in Immanuel Kant's (1724–1804) *Conflict of the Faculties.*[1] Kant was the leading philosopher of the eighteenth century. He revolutionized philosophy by exploring the limits of our minds to know. He was a champion of critical reasoning and inspired almost all the thinkers I've discussed, especially Hermann Cohen.

The idea of conflict among the schools or faculties is easy to see in the medieval university. It became a topic of reflection in Kant's work, which led to the complexity of our many-facultied universities. Historians have much to share with us (and to debate) about the origins of universities, but there's little dispute that they started with professional schools

– law in the Islamic context, law and theology in Italy, and theology throughout northern Europe. Long before there was a structure basic to the university, the higher faculties trained professionals, and the lower faculties focused on preparatory education. The lower faculty usually provided liberal arts training organized through a *trivium* (grammar, logic, rhetoric) and a *quadrivium* (arithmetic, geometry, music, astronomy). The liberal arts had a tradition going back to the Romans and even the Greeks, but they were delegated to a lower position in relation to the professional schools, called faculties.

Theology, law, and medical schools were bound to a variety of societal institutions, the church being the most important. The medieval church was complex and included diocesan authorities and various religious orders, and each profession emerged in complex tension with the church. The very term *profession* was associated with the profession of faith, and lawyers and doctors were often in clerical orders, with lawyers practising in church courts. Guilds for doctors and lawyers emerged from the twelfth through the fourteenth centuries, and they located the training of their professionals in the nascent universities.

In many cases, the professions did not require the creation of new knowledge; they depended on people learning old texts and old ways of reading. In other cases, inquiry and invention emerged as a key part of the university. Familiar arguments about the goals and shape of the university first appeared in these medieval contexts. The University of Paris was in turmoil for a time in the thirteenth century when the Dominican Order (to which Thomas Aquinas belonged) campaigned to excuse its students from the required studies of the lower faculties. The universities were international and though hardly secular in our sense, they were a place where some forms of study were negotiating specific freedoms from certain church authorities. In some ways, the plurality and conflict of the university reflected the commentary page and the complexity of premodern society, which had multiple estates and authorities.

Remember that during the Reformation, the conflicts became even more bitter. To gain some perspective on *more bitter*, the battles of church and state over education, especially university education, produced martyrs. The shifting alliances of churches and states produced wars and upheaval, some caused by learned debates about authority over the Bible or this-worldly and other-worldly success.

By the late eighteenth century, the university had come squarely under the control of the state, which licensed the university to grant degrees. The church and other professions were in competition with the emerging sciences, including philosophy. In 1792, Kant was censored by the state at the behest of the church. For Kant, the question became whether the church would control his ability to teach philosophy. But with respect to the university, it yielded what he called "a conflict of the faculties." Philosophy was the core of the lower faculties, having swallowed the trivium and quadrivium in its claim to govern all the sciences. Later, each science would gain its own independence and local foundation, but even when Kant divided the lower faculty into the historical and the pure, both were philosophy. The higher faculties were direct descendants of the medieval faculties, and theology was Kant's particular target. Kant also reflected on the relationship of philosophy to the faculties of law and medicine.

Most valuable for our purposes here, Kant claimed that there is a conflict that helps make the university what it is. In this conflict, philosophy is always challenging and being held in check. He was one of the thinkers who cherished the conflict that can't be resolved, making him a fit precursor of Lyotard and the idea of discord.

As a philosophical aside, Kant's idea of critique claimed that reason is fundamentally limited and so can never resolve some metaphysical debates (Does the world have a beginning, or is it eternal? Am I thoroughly mortal, or do I have an immortal soul?). Ironically, Kant's philosophical successors (including Schelling and Fichte) claimed to resettle much of the territory he proved inaccessible, conceiving a metaphysics of absolutes and totality and, appropriately, a university that could be absolutely unified.

Kant argued that the state controls the higher faculties (the professional schools), but the lower faculty (today's faculties of arts and sciences) should be left free to pursue truth so long as they don't meddle in the public sphere. The higher faculties serve the business of the state, which seeks to control people by guiding them in their health, property, and, ultimately, salvation – but they do not seek truth in itself.

Nonetheless, there is an intramural conflict between the higher and lower faculties, between authority and truth. Kant's immediate concern was academic freedom for the lower faculty, not for the higher.

Kant was disingenuous: in this model, he offers a view of the state contrary to his own political philosophy, which recognizes that truth and reason should lead society. He distinguishes between two sorts of university conflicts: illegal and legal. A legal conflict is about truth. Because Kant strangely sequesters inquiry and discovery in the lower faculty, the lower faculty can freely find the truth on any matter but can't publicize its findings. It must always obey the state. The professional schools, by contrast, labour to explain and expound on the state's decrees and traditions. They're not licensed to pursue the truth freely – they must operate within the bounds of what the state believes will enhance its authority and power. Within this context, illegal conflicts include pandering to interests external to the university and attacking reason and law to win public opinion.

The last century (even the last decade) has, alas, given us many examples of this kind of illegal conflict, cases where scholars are silenced for disagreeing with authorities or, as Lyotard warned, where terror is dominant.

As for the legal (or lawful) conflicts, for Kant, they can't be settled by mutual agreement because the lower faculty, in its pursuit of truth, must retain the chance to reach conclusions that conflict with government laws and regulations. Although the university might never challenge the government, the conflicts will be unending, resulting in constant progress in knowledge.

The issue that matters to us today is that some schools have an intrinsic relation to clients and societal bodies outside the university while some do not. This tension calls the university into existence. Ideas are in a dialogue that cannot be simply resolved or dissolved. The idea of freedom and the idea of responsibility are in a constructive and creative tension, different from their interplay in Kant but in some ways parallel.

Within professional schools, tension comes from the professors' need for freedom of inquiry. Professors engage in research, and the professions have little or no say in the choice of that research. Indeed, many professors claim a radical freedom to conduct research and inquiry along whatever path they want. All professors have a desire to do research in a manner Kant would have restricted to the arts and sciences. Clearly, questions about whether theologians can expound heresy and retain their teaching credentials are less central today. But law schools that fall afoul of a law society could still be denied accreditation. It would be rare, however, for a professor's research project to threaten the school's standing. An education professor might pursue research that rejects current norms for teaching or contest the state funding regime, but neither action would become a matter for review by a professional society.

Nonetheless, research informs and engages professional students, so there's a pull toward a body beyond the university, a sense of creating an education bound to others – to the profession and even the state.

In a contrary pull, arts and science professors want to be unbound from society – to be utterly autonomous. They believe that science – or, at least, the unbridled mind of the scientist –should set the agenda. Truth seems to be (and this, again, is the upshot of Kant's sleight of hand) exclusively theoretical. The professor can seek to know anything but does not act in the world.

This idea of freedom is and was (even in Kant's time) a caricature. In the social sciences, for instance, research often leads to advocacy for or even the implementation of significant policy changes. Some scientific research is closely allied to industry (or even the military). Some professors explore matters that will soon make a real change in society.

My key institutional point is that there are no mediating societies in the arts and sciences. Funders, often governmental bodies, may oversee and regulate research but frequently reserve substantial funds for basic research, allowing applicants to choose their own directions.

The state licenses the professional colleges and societies to regulate their members and the practices of the professional schools. The state is not an expert on engineering, medicine, or architecture, so it recognizes that experts should regulate the professions. A similar view is at work in the arts and sciences: legislators, judges, civil servants, and so on are not experts in cell biology, historical changes in the cultures of the Indian Ocean, or theoretical physics, so the state licenses the university to govern itself in intellectual matters. The university acts like its own professional body – it regulates itself by itself, usually collegially, even as it's training its future professors, taking us back to the dialogue between the ideas of replication and multiplication.

The tension between the ideas of freedom and responsibility has shifted overwhelmingly toward the idea of freedom – at least in the eyes of the professors. But this leaves arts and sciences faculties confused and vulnerable when they're confronted by demands for more accessible research or education in marketable skills. The professions serve clients who require specific services (for example, treatment of a toothache). But who do philosophers and physicists serve (beyond professional societies of philosophers or physicists)? Who, then, can make claims on the arts and sciences? Who outside the professoriate can represent a need, an interest, or a conviction about the value of an arts or sciences education?

Which raises one more thorny issue. As academics, professors belong to professional societies (societies that represent language professors, historians, physicists, economists, and philosophers) and larger interdisciplinary societies such as the Federation for the Humanities and Social Sciences, in Canada, or the American Council of Learned Societies, in the United States. Professional societies are not granted their authority to regulate by governmental licence, but they do censor and control what counts as a credential (one book or two articles?), and at conferences, academics learn what sorts of questions count as professional.

Ironically, our PhD programs are also highly professionalized – root curiosity and passion about our fields are disciplined and honed into expertise recognized by professors and professionals. When we think about the arts and sciences, we must not forget the strengths and limitations of the professional model of our professors – and it may well be that many of our graduates will profess philosophy or economics or chemistry in contexts beyond the university.

Each faculty finds an equilibrium between the idea of freedom and the idea of responsibility. But because these points differ, there's conflict among faculties. The university's funding and support is a major index of society's call, but professional councils, colleges, societies, and associations often call on the university to engage in the free inquiry that Kant used to characterize the lower faculties exclusively. Only by mapping the tension in each faculty and exploring the balance between freedom and responsibility more fully can we understand why governments and other social forces must support a range of equilibrium points.

Kant's account of the conflict of the faculties allows us to see that speculative unity is impossible and that self-regulation is not the only norm for the university. In place of an idea of unity – which would lead us to regard these basic conflicts of the faculties as the dissolution of the university – the idea of discord allows for a multiplicity of ways of doing research. The schools are not free to disregard one another. They share a common tension, but they negotiate it differently. The tension of the university is not simply opposition between teaching professional students and teaching liberal arts undergraduates; rather, it's a doubling of discord, within each faculty and then between them.

What makes a set of faculties that hold a range of ideas about their relation to society into a university will be ongoing conversation and negotiation. Research universities gain much by connecting with the professions. But we do not want to restrict the university to medical, business, and law schools. We need a model that tolerates and encourages diversity while fostering debates and conversations that revise the balance or equilibrium between responsibility and freedom.

The idea I appropriated from Lyotard in the last chapter can now be extended to this nonunitary but not dismembered set of schools. This idea, however, requires more exploration, because whether we set professional schools against the arts and sciences or pit the professions against independent inquiry, we have yet to reach a clear account of how students learn in relation to these tensions. If, as Lyotard suggests, the goal is to seek connections that do not yet exist – to explore a future that is not merely the unification of all disciplines, professions, and sciences – then the university's task is shaped by this ongoing inquiry and the creation of links across diverse fields of study.

Questions Come from Others

So far, I've drawn a map of schools, each of which balances the tension between the claims of society and the freedom of inquiry. It is now clear that even professors of philosophy are licensed by the state to provide a university education. For some critical thinkers, this structure (in which the dominant agent with power such as the church, the state, or global capital can create a space for a self-legislating institution) only undermines the foundational claims of that institution. No research university has freedom or self-governance of the absolute or metaphysical sort. Nor do the professions with their professional societies exercise control absolutely. University education happens in a negotiated and negotiating environment characterized by conflicting ideas.

What kind of student thinking does university education cultivate in relation to these tensions of freedom and responsibility? What does it mean to learn in the context of a dialogue between independent inquiry and responsibility to society? Let's look again at the thinking students can learn to see how the dialogue between freedom and responsibility is part of inquiry and critique. What is the epistemological and personal reality of this dialogue?

We can assume that when an idea of freedom guides the university, the goal is to teach the student to think for herself. Unsettling settled knowledge is a call to self-reflection that leads to the discovery that her own thinking, her judgment on matters, is truly in her power. University education not only teaches her a tradition or a body of material, but it also teaches her to think it through, reorganize it, or dismiss some aspects of it. She learns to ask questions, which may well be the heart of learning how to do research. She finds her own questions. This allows her to become free of the past and to form herself in the present as judge and knower. Such is the university's task under the idea of freedom.

Now, contrast that with the idea of responsibility, where the student is taught how to think in response to others. In instruction on settled matters, he receives knowledge from others (in person, in books, or online). But in university education, he learns to reflect in a way that answers to others. It is their questions that drive him to doubt the familiar narrative. Of course, the other may tell him what to think and may claim to dominate him, but if he discerns the way another person calls him to think, he may have arrived at the heart of education: not told what to think, not simply thinking for himself, but thinking at their call, for another or on their behalf – responding to another. A call to answer is not merely a call to regurgitate information, as in a Google search, but to suit one's thinking to the person asking. To respond.

I also distinguish thinking for oneself from thinking by oneself. In the modern period of reading, one reads by oneself. One writes by oneself. True, I also admit that one reads in groups and shares drafts and, indeed, converses and thinks in the company of other people. The story used to be that education helped a person become a free individual while studying in the social context of others who were engaging in the same kind of learning: each person was learning to think for themselves. But the assumption that haunts even this social account of thinking is that each of us relates to the truth separately. But what if truth depends on relating with others or through others?

I'll make extensive use here of a remarkable letter, a letter that marks a break from the German university by the Jewish philosopher Franz Rosenzweig (1886–1929). Rosenzweig was from a liberal Jewish community. After completing a major work, *Hegel and the State*, he turned to Jewish philosophy, studying with Hermann Cohen and writing one of the masterpieces of modern Jewish thought, *The Star of Redemption*.[2] He was a leader of the Jewish Renaissance between the wars in Germany and died from ALS in 1929.

Rosenzweig declined a rare chance for a Jew to become a professor in Germany. I'll say more about his turn away from the university, but I want to start with a blunt and important statement of the issues as he saw them: "I ask only, where *I am being asked.* Asked by a person [*Mensch*], and not from the scholar, not from 'science' [*Wissenschaft*]."[3]

For Rosenzweig, the university was trapped in its confidence that scholars were carrying on scholarship or science and that *science* demanded, science requested, science needed to know, and so on. Rosenzweig rejected the claim that he should think for the sake of science, and he refused to assert that he needed to know for himself. He did not regard his independence from tradition as the touchstone of learning and inquiry. No, he was willing to think, learn, and teach only when another person asked him. He revealed that learning is, most of all, bound up with other people, and learning is not like an assembly line where each person does the same task side by side or as successive tasks that build knowledge products. No, learning is facing another and responding. What sets us to think and learn are other people's questions.

Here, we've moved to a new existential insight into the future of university education. Can the university teach students how to respond to the questions asked by others? Is this a cast of mind, habit, or way of thinking that can be taught?

If we wish to emphasize the two moments (research and unsettling reflection) that we've identified as university education, we need to ask how each relates to thinking for oneself and thinking in response to another. In Chapter 3, we saw that the goal of promoting unsettling reflection has changed because each discipline now tries to justify its own knowledge locally. Each student is learning how to juxtapose, question, and balance diverse fields, seeing the specific ways one learns and comes to know in each field. Because the unity of all knowledge is no longer sought in a single mind, universities benefit from creating contexts where students learn with other students. This is not a simple opposition between loyalty to one method and aiming to compile a unified encyclopedia in one mind. Rather, something about the differences and gaps allows one to call to the other. This, I would suggest, is the benefit of having many departments and fields in the arts and sciences – the goal isn't to learn many disciplines but to learn how learning happens in many disciplines and to learn how to learn with others.

In many ways, professional schools accept plurality in learning. Students aren't exposed to a diversity of fields, but the inclusion of practitioners as teachers in the schools' programs opens new questions and perspectives. More than practicums where students apprentice or clerk or intern, the professional programs include practitioners who have access to questions from clients that call for a different sort of thinking by students.

Questions originate not in abstract realms but from people, indeed, from specific individuals. Rosenzweig doubted the university could heed those questioners. But fellow students are a rich source of questions. Students in the innovation class learned from one another what each person wanted to learn. As we found in Chapter 2, heeding students' questions reverses the flow of inquiry: education shifts from instructing students to students learning how to learn in response to one another's questions. For someone who is not an expert, the esoteric nature of developed scientific discourse provokes unsettling questions. The goal of instruction, then, is to register and refine those questions. The less expert students become the people for whom the professors think. The professors model and teach all students to think in response to others. Here, we've returned to Humboldt's vision of the lecture, but now questions from another person are provoking thought. By focusing on questions, communication is restored as the essence of education.

According to the idea of freedom, this focus on student questions is contrary to education's task because the goal of thinking for myself is finding the relation between my mind and the truth. Within the task of thinking for myself, communication is a secondary activity that involves relaying knowledge I already hold, knowledge that is already established and past.

But communication in this new scenario is not delivering information, nor is it the transmission of tradition. It is being exposed to another person's questions. It is a call from another person to think in an open future.

Students with questions are representatives of society. Even when there's no mediating professional body, their education can explore how we come to discern the limits of what is known. This is learning how to respond to the questions of nonscholars, of those in society who are not in the university. "Why do we need to know this method?" "How can we be sure of this claim?" "How does what we know about one thing fit with our knowledge about something else or about our knowledge in a course in another field?" When other students embody and give voice to such questions, the questions reach out beyond the hypothetical.

If learning to respond to others' questions is a goal of university education, then the university needs to teach students to listen for questions and help clarify what is being asked. Teaching, then, shows students to welcome questions and teachers to welcome and multiply inquiry. Thinking in response to another is more than giving an answer – it's thinking that clarifies and explores the question. It's learning from the practices of heeding and responding.

If we classify student questions as critical and regard learning how to hear and respond to them as valuable, then we can progress to the education that occurs in learning to do research. Where do the questions for research come from? Are we teaching researchers to think for themselves or to think in response to others?

If I were to take the stance that I, as a professor, should have the freedom to explore whatever question I like, to research topics of my choosing, using methods that I adopt or revise, then we can readily see that learning to think for myself is a core value. No one gets to tell the professor what to research.

And yet ... in the process of peer review or tenure review, other professors regulate research. Someone can still surprise his field with a new finding or a new question, but legitimation comes with adhering to the canons of argument: otherwise, the finding or question will not count as valid and may not make it to publication. In this sense, science does ask the research questions – that is, professors in the field delimit questions and methods. Recall the role of academic societies: they are groups of experts who legitimate certain sorts of research. Similarly, funding also is determined by external bodies and professors.

Rosenzweig addressed the existential aspect of research in this letter explaining why he was abandoning the university to found an adult education program:

> Knowing remains free in itself when it lets no one prescribe its *answers*. Never the *answers*, but the *questions* (and here is my heresy against the unwritten fundamental law of the University). For me, not every question is worthy of being asked. Scientific curiosity, like an aesthetic hunger for food, held me under its spell – but today it no longer fills me. I ask only, where *I am being asked*. Asked by a person [*Mensch*], and not from the scholar, not from "science" [*Wissenschaft*]. But even in the scholar a human is hiding, an asker who is answer-worthy. In the scholar's humanity: but no longer in the *science* in the scholar.
>
> Scholarship: that inexhaustible curious insatiable gluttonous spectre, which possesses him, and consumes him until nothing of his humanity remains. I hate this spectre like all spectres. For me, its questions are no questions. But the questions of people have become more compelling. For them, as much as I can, I commit to answer and as much as I know – from a limited knowledge and thus limited ability.[4]

There is an essential freedom in knowing, and it comes from the thinking and from the way the answers cannot be dictated in advance. If a funder or a professor asks someone to do research but stipulates the result, this is not research. The crookedness violates protocol, but it also violates how learning and thinking work. A researcher seeking new knowledge is a skilled seeker, not merely a panderer or propagandist. The mind fastens on novelty and delights in seeing something that had been unseen. The rigour of research allows one to set off from settled shores or even from charted paths. The destination is uncertain and often unknown. Exploring has its risks, but inquiry is fundamentally different from settling in a surveyed space. Well and good. The desire to learn and to know, the curiosity of the scholar, is a great thing. No one can stipulate the answers – if they do, it's not knowledge, nor is it research.

According to Rosenzweig, the university has a fundamental law: science alone gets to ask questions. He claimed he had to leave the university because he wished to make the university open to the people who ask, who call him to respond.

I took this claim as a challenge by trying to imagine a university that does respond. A task of this book is to reinvigorate the research university and to imagine it open to other questioners. What Rosenzweig held to be impossible – that the research university would yield absolute control of the questions – is here something to be considered.

In the longer quotation from Rosenzweig's letter, however, we see the scientist and researcher emerge as people who also ask questions. They also ask one another, and the questions are worthy of answering precisely in relation to the person asking, not their knowledge, expertise, or status. Rosenzweig's sad, if eloquent, charge is that the truly free inquiry of the scholar will eat up all his humanity, the worthy asker, leaving a mere ghost of a person. Why does this person now care about this research? Where is her passion that posed the research question in the first place? This passion was more than a general desire to know but rather a specific desire that aggravated her with a specific problem, a challenge, that took the form of an insufficiency of current knowledge. Can we imagine research that does not train us to lose sight of why it matters to someone? I challenge Rosenzweig by imagining a model for a university that teaches students how to do research, claiming that this education will be more likely to refresh the researcher's humanity than a research environment with the highest levels of self-regulation.

From this doubt about Rosenzweig's fundamental law, I return to two tasks for the research-intensive university: undergraduate research and professional student research. The inexpert undergraduate offers ready access to critical thinking. And undergraduates and professional students, in different ways, point us to research methods that could be more attuned to people's questions. Undergraduate students' connections to the world around them, along with their newly developed habit of questioning knowledge, make more immediately relevant the question, Why does this matter? Learning the skills to develop a question into a research project is a task for university education, and in the strongest sense, this can be learning to think in response to another. The student not only answers for herself but learns how to be asked and how to pursue questions that matter to others.

In professional programs, moreover, because the professions work with many people beyond the university, the need to heed questions and seek new knowledge driven by personal concerns and passions is essential. In this sense, a council, college, or society may govern a profession and represent the profession to the university, but the clients (the beneficiaries of the professionals) are the focus of the profession. *If we could control Type 2 diabetes, or reduce diphtheria, or spread literacy, or protect intellectual property, or ...* I hope you recognize this list as goals and questions that have already been addressed by researchers in the professions. Personal questions guide research in the professions, and the university plays a central role in conducting that research and even more in educating professionals to strive to answer those questions.

The questions that framed this chapter have once again opened a radical inquiry into ideas that expand our view of the university. We began with a view where the university's responsibility to society could easily be reduced to mere accountability or economic return on investment. That responsibility might also be framed as a duty to meet labour market needs, support national security or prosperity, or serve political interests. In this view, the university's unifying principle could be a shared funding model, a foundation for science progress, or even a grounding in ethics for all students.

I can say, moreover, that this more limited idea of responsibility is still in play here in the view I'm proposing. The practice of hearing the questions can bring insight to those initial concerns. Students who learn how to do research, how to listen to others and think in response to questions brought by another, are the most highly prized sorts of minds in our society – a society in which new questions emerge with great force and people need help finding new answers and new kinds of knowledge.

Nonetheless, the path we are travelling in this book is uncommon, most of all because it tries to discern the distinctive features of a student's learning. I've brought us to a point where the university is called not to answer to itself, or even to answer for itself, but to answer questions that come from another person. The professional schools already have access to and a commitment to answering those questions. Practical instruction or vocational training is front-line training in responding to the questions of others whereas university education is more reflective and, indeed, innovative in learning how to heed the questions. Undergraduate arts and sciences students might seem to be absorbing knowledge and information, but the real task of the university is to help them learn to heed the unsettling questions and, beyond that, to develop the discipline and creativity to respond to questions that call for new knowledge and new views of unsettled matters. The research university, thus, can teach by welcoming students' questions.

The privilege I'm extending to these students and their education is itself a reflection of society's call to the university. Although there are many PhD students and professors, undergraduates in the arts and sciences and professional students (long unrecognized) make up the vast preponderance of the university population. In 2023, the University of Toronto had almost 100,000 full- and part-time students. Undergraduate arts and sciences students numbered 58,000, and professional master's and undergraduate students numbered 27,000. Smaller but still large universities have vast numbers of professional students. This statistical reality is not news to university administrators. This book doesn't offer yet another set of programs and strategic enrolment plans. It's a way of thinking about the inherent discord and opening our eyes to the fact that universities are already deeply engaged in research that arises from our responsibility to society.

But, again, we need to inquire about what kind of thinking the students could be learning.

Let's take one more paragraph from Rosenzweig's letter because it also addresses how the following questions animate thinking: What is knowledge? What is it for? Who is it for?

> For me knowledge is no longer an end in itself. It has become service for me. Service for people *certainly not* (Don't misunderstand me!) as service to a bias or an agenda ("*Tendenz*"). Biases are for me more than hateful; I believe they are impossible for knowledge.
>
> Knowing remains free in itself, when it lets no one prescribe its *answers*. Never the *answers* ... But the *questions* ... (and here is my heresy against the unwritten fundamental law of the University). For me, not every question is worthy of being asked.[5]

This passage, which directly introduces the passage I've been quoting and requoting, makes a claim that should not be shocking but is nevertheless disturbing. It takes us to the heart of my opening question, What is university education for? Knowledge becomes a mode of service, serving people.

This idea set off alarms because it could run the risk of becoming slavish, of making thinking a tool or instrument for another's agenda. The history of universities and the sciences is filled with examples of universities acting in disciplined service to the nation, the church, the state, the colonial empire, the global capital order, and to a people. The idea of freedom responds to and advances a critique against this type of bias, against coercion.

But Rosenzweig argued that this idea of freedom is not adequate. Knowledge is not an end in itself and need not deteriorate into a mere tool. Knowing exercises finite freedom in the service of specific people – not in the service of the nation, the economy, or knowledge itself. Because the powers that be might demand obedience and try to force inquiry and results, the idea of freedom can help professors champion learning to think for oneself, inquiry as something that can stand independent of such forces. The epistemology of thinking for myself, moreover, relies on a single mind thinking in the present moment in direct relation to the truth. The idea of responsibility sees knowledge as service; it balances being vulnerable to people who ask questions with a thinking for the future that depends on and maintains a social relation.

The idea of discord helps us see that conflicts and equilibriums among the faculties reflect the unresolvable dialogue between freedom of inquiry and responsibility to society. From there, we can see that a research university is a complex set of practices based on learning to think for the sake of and with others. Skill in welcoming questions – in attending to students and society, to questions that matter to someone – instigates inquiry. The research university's responsibility is to educate students of all sorts to think and to inquire in a way that is open to the future question, to the next student who brings a worthy question.

5

Connecting Universities to Cities and Communities

Students flow through the university over a few short years. Except during the pandemic lockdowns, they flow into and out of the campus almost daily. So far, I've drawn on my experiences at the University of Toronto, but I also had a residential fellowship at the University of British Columbia, where I delivered John V. Clyne Lectures, which formed the backbone of this book.

I turn here specifically to UBC's students. There are approximately sixty thousand students enrolled at the Vancouver campus. Due to political negotiations made over a century ago, the campus is located on a beautiful promontory on the ocean, a thirty- to forty-five-minute drive from downtown Vancouver and at least an hour-and-a-half bus ride from the populous and more affordable suburbs.

Outside of the pandemic years, one might well assume that UBC students are on campus, studying. But where do they live? We talk about "attending" university, and UBC has room for twelve thousand students in residence. The university claims bragging rights to having the most student residential places at a Canadian university, but the numbers are not dramatically different from other major Canadian universities. For instance, the University of Toronto can house ten thousand students.

The more significant point is the small number of residents in relation to the total number of students. At an Ivy League school, close to 100 percent of students live in residence, and some of the big public universities in the United States have a high percentage of students living in dorms. In many other countries and cities, by contrast, students commute.

So where do the students at UBC live? Recent survey data indicate that while almost half of first-year undergraduates live on the campus, the number shrinks to 10 percent in fourth-year. Perhaps the key indicator of *where* they are is time spent commuting: fourth-year students spent 6.3 hours per week, and the average for all students was eleven hours or more per week. UBC has bragging rights on another metric: the longest average commute for students. But, again, other major Canadian universities are close. Many students live at home with their families, parents, and sometimes extended family members. There are social and economic reasons for these arrangements.

So it seems that much of the time the students are on the bus. UBC has a great transit pass, U-Pass BC. York University in Toronto has a new connection on the subway. In most cities, transit support and access are part of being a student. Of course, the implications of these distances and travel times are multiple. According to a UBC survey data of undergraduates, 70 percent of students participate in fewer than five hours per week of cocurricular activities – including sports, organizations, publications, and so on.

In universities around the world, there has been extensive discussion of and investment in what is called "the student experience," focusing on what universities provide when students are *not* in class. But given these commuting times, there are serious limitations on how engaged students can be. (Frankly, this is an issue for most large public universities in most countries.) The assumption is that when students live at home, spend time on the bus, and work at a job they are somehow missing out on the real experience of university education. The idea is that students should live in isolation from the world (including from their parents) and its many claims upon their time. The ideal of universities as providing a place where students live and play, where social life outside the classroom is curated for them, serves only a few Canadian universities, but it dominates the US and English university systems.

What if we turn the university inside out? In this final chapter, I offer a different look at the student experience by exploring the educational benefits of the urban commuter university – common in Canada and much of Europe, Latin America, Asia, and other parts of the world. Students learn in two places (in their home communities and the university), offering a way for research to act as a bridge as students attend to society's questions and bring questions to the city to learn. I call this an urban epistemology – the ways of knowing that emerge through interactions between a university and its surrounding city. These exchanges go beyond viewing the city merely as an object of study; they also recognize the city's inhabitants as active participants in knowledge creation, working alongside university members as collaborators. The university provides students with places to study (study spaces) and to draw insight from their commuting.

My wager is that something is learned best in a congregated location, in meetings that happen in real time and real space – and on that wager, the future of the university may ride. After experiencing online education during the pandemic, we understand there are good reasons to come together at the university and that there's real potential for learning in the to and fro of the city.

An Urban Epistemology

Education and the student experience occur in close proximity. We need a new and more honest account of the student experience, one that carefully considers how students live and study at large urban universities. The ideal assumes a care-free campus where students live. It assumes students who do not need to work or travel. We need to widen our assumptions about what the student experience should be. Moreover, I'm interested in asking how different ways of living might enhance the possibilities for their education.

The University of Toronto, the Université de Montréal, or the University of British Columbia look a lot more like one another than they do, say, Cambridge or Princeton. In Canada, we teach students in metropolitan cities. We teach students who live in Toronto, Montreal, and Vancouver but not at university. In the Canadian system, most undergraduates live in their home communities. Add in the National University of Singapore, Sapienza University of Rome, Humboldt University of Berlin, and the University of Sydney in Australia, and we would quickly see that large urban research universities require a different model. How do we understand the kind of learning that is possible for students who live off-campus in Canada's uncommonly diverse cities and, more broadly, in the metropolitan environments of cities worldwide?

To focus on where students live, I sketch three general models of student experience. First, we have a university with a residential campus. Students live in dorms. They've moved away from their families and usually from their home communities, creating a society of people who are almost all the same age and away from their parents' authority. It is a time of freedom from supervision and surveillance. This model prevails in elite universities in some systems and often dominates discussions of what a university should be. The university is responsible for curating the activities of students outside of class.

Second, we have an urban campus where students live in the city, often in a given quarter. They live with other students but not on the grounds of the university and not with their parents. Social relations are more heterogeneous than in the campus model, and fewer people are watching out for these students. This model fits many European universities.

Third, we have an urban university where students live at home and commute. They may move out of their parental home into their home community, but they remain local. Students can easily stay in touch with their high school friends and are more likely to settle later near their homes. This is the Canadian system, which is common in other countries.

Of course, much has been written recently about the student experience, but I'll again turn to Schleiermacher to lay out the stakes for these three models.[1] Schleiermacher acts as a guide because he reflected profoundly on the link between the goals of university education and moral development. Under the idea of freedom, university education is learning to think for yourself about knowledge. Such thinking can't be forced with penalties or lashes. The suspension of supervision or surveillance means suspending control over external actions such as dress and manners.

The student experience was a key part of debates at the founding of the University of Berlin. Schleiermacher discussed activities such as drinking, gambling, duelling and, of course, sex. His arguments about the student experience included descriptions of rambunctious youths who did not attend university and the students who were faddish – dressing and drinking in groups, each just like the other. In short, the students shared a form of urban fraternity.

Schleiermacher argued that the emancipation of the mind required being free from constraints. He noted and approved unregulated student schedules, with no one forcing them to go to bed, wake up, or go to class. The temporality of study and learning is a recurrent theme in *Occasional Thoughts of Universities in the German Sense,* and freedom of thought creates its own time and rhythm. Hence our interest in slowing down reading in Chapter 3.

There are many distractions from the challenges of thinking and, in part, the distractions depend on where a student lives. While in high school, students spent most of their time in class or doing homework. Course time is much less in university (with fewer contact hours), and few students expect that their time outside of class will be one continuous round of studying.

For students living on campus in the first model, social distractions focus on fellow students – clubs, sports, dining halls, literary journals, political activism, campus services, drinking rites, music, and drama. Impromptu conversations happen at meals, parties, in the library, and at organized events. The US model projects an image of a generally carefree time. *Time management* means creating a social network and getting the most out of these few short years (often described as "the best years of your life"). Expectations on a student's time are reduced well below what you'd normally experience while working a job or practising a profession. And no one's the boss of you. Universities labour to create a range of noncurricular activities and the comfort of enjoying them. They're stepping up support for the mental health of students struggling in this novel environment. In elite contexts, we expect universities to provide distractions and study – and much of the experience revolves around high-end facilities that create an almost country club or summer camp environment.

In the second model, the distractions come from the excitement and culture of the city – for us, this would be theatre, film, books, pubs, music, activism, and politics. We could argue that students inject creativity and energy into this cultural life – not only as consumers but also as producers. Politics and direct engagement with the social struggles of the city are readily accessible to these city dwellers. The university has little responsibility (and in Schleiermacher's day, it was felt that it took too little care) for what students get up to when not studying. If the students represent a wider range of social classes, then a main use of their time will be working. While the campus has extensive settings for interaction, the city offers interactions with a more varied community. Meals are either fast food from local outlets or made at home, and organized activities are not as readily available as on campus. Time outside of class tends to be in the hands of the student.

In the third model, students live in their home communities and often have responsibilities to their families and friends from high school. Many are working (and some are working a lot). Indeed, most are working to attend university, which raises the question, What does it mean to be a full-time university student? It rarely means students are spending all their time in classes and studying. When students live at home, they often have ongoing social events and networks. Whether through parties, sports, family obligations, music, or religious practices, connections with home communities place demands on students' time and provide opportunities to engage in activities outside the university setting, depending on one's perspective. The community may be culturally homogeneous but diverse in terms of age and education. Time is more flexible than in high school, and students may have more control over bedtime and waking time, but they are living with more claims on their time than on-campus students.

Schleiermacher's model was the second one, where students live in the city but not at home. He claimed that if the students didn't get the freedom to engage in extracurriculars, they would not have the internal discipline and desire to learn the new kinds of questioning that characterize university education. He contrasted school (where the teacher directs learning) with the university (where the student grows to direct his own education, eventually designing new research and creating new knowledge). The goal was to displace obedience and the cane with internal judgment, which is disciplined by philosophical thought. In Schleiermacher's model, schools and parents (and the church and other civil society institutions) treat younger children almost as objects or mere animals, capable of obedience but not self-governance. All the more reason to have a period of radical doubt and reconsolidation of the intellectual order, mirroring doubt in the moral order. We can assume that licence in the moral sphere is derived from educational goals. But perhaps finding moral norms for yourself (even if they're the traditional ones) matches the activity of finding the intellectual unity of (but not abandoning) all science. This short period of questioning allows a person to become more productive and even more obedient in one's adult years. Normality requires, says the modern bourgeois thinker, a measure of formal independence.

From the viewpoint of the idea of freedom, the student's biography begins with their earlier years of schooling, when they're living at home in a stage of coercion, dependence, and surveillance. Moving out of home begins a new stage of freedom, which is central to learning to think for yourself. Of course, in the process, some students will fail both morally and intellectually, but the risk is justified because obedience and fear are not adequate for creative research or a full social life.

Moral development in the first (campus) model rests on a lack of surveillance coupled with a vast range of facilities and programs. Potential issues include *in loco parentis*, sexual harassment, hazing and fraternity life, multiple sorts of psychological challenges, and, of course, the extensive costs of providing suitable accommodation and programming, costs often borne by the students or their families.

To refocus on students in the urban contexts of Canada, Singapore, Italy, and elsewhere, let's focus on the third model. What is the moral frame and parallel intellectual task of the university in a city such as Vancouver, Toronto, Montreal, Manchester, Seoul, or Rome? Is there an ethics of social relations here that is embodied by civil society, one that values a range of connections that Schleiermacher's bourgeois overlooks?

Within the idea of responsibility, making a break from childhood, parents, and local community is not viewed as the sole or even the best path to maturity. In this story of ethical and intellectual growth, much depends on learning how to respond to other people's questions, on how to think in response to others. Here, the opposition between obedience and independence is impoverished. To be responsible is not merely to be obedient. How do we learn how to be responsive and attend to others? If our deepest insights into good will come from listening to others, if our highest principles can only be found in a complicated matrix of responsibilities, if new moral insights take place in interaction with long lines of tradition, then the premise that we must move out and sever relations with family and community to find our moral direction might be inadequate.

Of course, in this third model many a student will feel limited and thwarted seeing their family every day, but there's also an ethics that sees that close contact at this age will allow the student to draw positive insight and ethical maturity from their responsibility toward others. Are we sure that maturity can only be found carousing with same-age students? If there's a positive role for home communities to play at this age, then total independence might come at a great cost.

Before I turn to the educational tasks that match this social reality, let me add that the tension between work and study is not necessarily worse than that between play and study. The ideas I'm exploring recognize that university education is not reducible to job training. Our students work to study. They sacrifice time and money for the sake of university education; thus, working can be seen as a moral task and not purely as a distraction. Less-skilled jobs in food services, retail, offices, and so on are a means to an end; they reflect the students' responsibility to themselves and their families, who can't afford to clothe, feed, and cover tuition.

A student experience not based on leisure can embody ethical norms. Upper-class privilege is not identical here with studying at university. Isn't an economic negotiation for the sake of education a key step in moral development, a kind of taking responsibility? Canadian students are serious about their studies. They are not in university to have fun, fun, fun. And they are not going to university to escape their parents' homes, values, and traditions – well, not simply. They do not have the same sense of leisure often associated with the ideal of campus life, but a student who lives in the city, and so is engaged daily with people in their community, may well have richer opportunities to communicate their studies beyond the university.

Let's add in the idea of permeability. The university should engage with society through the flow of knowledge, questions, and, of course, students.

THE IDEA OF PERMEABILITY. The ability to permit flow across, through, or between two beings. In the university, this is the flow of students (and others) through the institution and, specifically, the flow from society in and out of the university.

Many kinds of systems are self-regulating without being self-enclosed; indeed, without flow, there would be nothing there (this works for living things most of all, but also for other kinds of systems, including information systems and economies). Identity is not rigid; it's responsive. Most important, a person learns not by being built up into a structure, turned into a machine or edifice, but by letting things flow through them.

The goal of university education is learning how to let the questions flow in to irrigate the fields of knowledge and tradition and instigate new insights and solutions. The idea of permeability suggests how university education can match the students' socially embedded experience by connecting study to home.

This model has two places for student life: the home community and the university. In the final section, I'll take up the specific value of the university as a place, but in this section, I reflect on what living at home offers university education. Most importantly, I want to think about commuting itself as a facet of university education.

The tension between society and the university now happens in space as the student commutes between the two places. In Chapter 4, this tension appeared between the universities and the professions and in the nature of thinking, in the sense that thinking is responding to another person, which requires the freedom to follow the inquiry wherever it might go. What does the pull toward the home community represent in the student's life?

For many, the social bonds of home (which are fraught, as all familiar and strong bonds are) are a call to succeed, excel, and satisfy other people's expectations. Class mobility is key. For many recent immigrants, the university represents the parent's dream for the student, a chance to gain new status or higher income but also to allow their child's mind to flourish. Social bonds also represent a call to respond. Many parents and other members of the home community want to know what a student is learning. There's a great conviction that a university education can lead to a fuller or better life. Often, during the undergraduate years, there's negotiation and alteration as the student discovers new kinds of study, new paths, or new professions or callings that diverge from the purpose the parents had prescribed for the university. Is it always better to negotiate by moving out rather than by living with your parents?

These intense and specific expectations lead the student to explain the purpose of their university education. For many students, there's intense communication with home (even those who live on campus are often online with their families daily). This call from home, beyond the barest social norms, is a form of questioning, and does not university education teach us to attend to, refine, develop, and explore questions?

If a student is only receiving schooling – acquiring information and advanced settled knowledge that is over the heads of their parents – what they're learning may or may not be easily communicable. But this is not the stuff of university education. When the student is learning how to think critically and to doubt and rethink settled information, their studies should be communicable, not only to professors and to fellow students but also to their friends and family.

Often, professors in the humanities suggest that students share drafts of their papers with family or friends to see if the writing is making sense. The student can learn to hear and respond to the society of questions that exists outside the university, prompting her to seek new knowledge and new perspectives. Questions can arise from societal challenges rooted in local realities, even when the most pressing issues – such as the shrinking of the Great Barrier Reef, regional conflicts in Ukraine and Gaza, or broader wars and social revolutions – are happening elsewhere. These events still resonate with and impact people at the local level. In short, living in the home community can intensify the student's engagement by making them aware of the need to communicate what they are thinking and learning at the university. Attention to what matters outside the university is key to a theory of knowledge that moves beyond appropriation of settled matters to questioning and learning how to think in response to others.

There's also a flipside to the questions coming from the home communities. Once we recognize that students are learning in these two places, we can imagine the research university attending to society's questions but also bringing its own questions to the city. With the idea of permeability, we see that communication can go in both directions, if not symmetrically then at least in an exchange. We can imagine a process where the whole city, with its diverse communities and societal bodies, engages with the university through its students. Indeed, we know that in many of the professions, the university has long brought practitioners into the university and sent students out as interns. So universities are already modelling this type of flow.

Over the last years, there has been a proliferation of programs to engage universities with their cities: outreach lectures where professors present their findings or policy suggestions; internships for students to gain experience working in specific, often professional, contexts; and cooperatives that offer students a focused learning environment. There are universities dedicated to this kind of learning: the University of Guelph in Ontario, Northeastern University in Massachusetts, and most medical schools.

For our purposes, I focus on community-exchange research models, which are more complex. In many places, Indigenous studies programs no longer focus on Indigenous cultures and peoples as objects of study but rather as partners in inquiry. The Indigenous law program at the University of Victoria, which I mentioned earlier, is one of a growing number of law programs in which law students participate and learn how to do research in exchange contexts. Similarly, the EPICS program at Purdue, which has an international network, has included society partners in engineering education for over twenty years. As a field, geography is remarkably well suited to research in dialogue with societal partners, which is happening in universities from Flinders in Australia to Bournemouth in England. And, of course, research in new information technologies engages in partnerships and includes undergraduates at diverse universities. MIT has led the way in research exchanges for this and other scientific fields.

The research focus of these initiatives is distinct from the current high-profile emphasis on entrepreneurship, but teaching students how to inquire in both university and society may well extend to placements and inquiry with industrial partners or governments. These placements, partnerships, co-ops, and internships all represent a desire to let society and universities engage and advance inquiry together.

At the Jackman Humanities Institute, we had several international initiatives. Our most successful was a third research community in partnership with the University of the Western Cape (UWC) in South Africa. From the University of Toronto side, the community included approximately forty professors from seven faculties. Titled "Aesthetic Education: A South-North Dialogue," its goal was to build a lasting partnership – and that takes much time. The topics of inquiry were various (puppetry, museums and public history, truth and reconciliation commissions, and so on). The goal was to explore how university education is local by contrasting two universities. How did each university engage their students' home communities? Once again, we looked for contrasts in part to discern the limitations of each urban university. Because the partnership at the University of Toronto was diverse and cross-cutting, only the Jackman Humanities Institute could convene and host it at the early stage. We wanted to do more than just create research couples. We wanted to learn something about our own local practices and those of UWC.

The primary, and still striking, discovery was that the humanities in South Africa were much more energized and connected to local communities and their histories. The question that arose at UWC, especially at its Centre for Humanities Research, was, What is a post-apartheid university? Thanks to attentive scholars and administrators, UWC had space to hear the call to work with communities in the city and the neighbouring Cape Flats. Like the Maori research centre in New Zealand, Ngā Pae o te Māramatanga, also a federally funded centre of research excellence, the Centre for Humanities Research received a federal grant to host "The Flagship on Critical Thought in African Humanities."

This funding, in contrast to our funding crises in North America, pointed to a quite different image of the humanities, especially its research. The New Zealand government recognized supporting "inside out" research exchanges as part of a commitment to fostering a different role for the university.

The communities of the Cape Flats and Indigenous nations had long been excluded from universities or, at best, studied as objects of research. These communities put forward dramatic and radical questions about how the research university could open itself to learning along with people who lived in the neighbourhood. One hugely successful partnership was the Handspring Puppet Company, which provided the puppets for the theatre hit *War Horse*. The partnership brought together students, faculty, and communities to explore telling and creating stories in any medium but most often in the form of festivals and pageants. The university helped guide the process, which required paying creative attention and listening to the local community's and the students' experiences.

The idea of permeability can help us think about how commuting students are a medium of communication. Spatially, they are in motion, moving from home to the university and from university back home. What if epistemology, the theory of knowledge itself, were to embrace these circular paths or flows to reconceive learning and inquiry? Knowledge is not something merely built up in an edifice but rather something that moves between people and different spheres of society. What counts as a good question in your home community might be less valued in the university and vice versa.

Commuting students provide a model for communicating university education because they allow for exchange in both directions. Instead of disconnecting the activities of university education from society, the urban university could embrace commuting as a way to engage diverse communities of expertise, traditional knowledge, and ongoing research. This embrace would include welcoming a flow of questions and learning from outside the university; it would aim to teach students how to share not their knowledge so much as their new ways of thinking.

What we know we communicate. Listening, reflecting, and responding are all profoundly bound to one another. The placements and research exchange programs I gesture to here are resources for rethinking how to teach students in relation to this idea of permeability. This urban epistemology is underway. The idea of permeability can be used to draw together and extend existing programs. Moreover, we can set a goal of providing research-intensive education at scale, where the research university actively engages with society and positions students as the key agents in this connection. Research universities play a unique role in shaping how we think, equipping students to develop the practices of thinking, and, in doing so, becoming more responsive (more permeable) to the needs of the world.

Study Space

But why would students value coming to campus? What makes a place of learning valuable? Interestingly, recognizing that students are predominantly commuters presumes they do not stay home. Even in the dark time of the pandemic, there was a widespread desire to go to campus. The strength of the home community connection does not outweigh the benefits of commuting, of travelling back and forth to the university. Students desire a place to study.

The value of study is balanced against the value of practice, of doing. Why spend three to four or even seven to ten years in university studying when one could just get on with it – whether "it" is making money, organizing a social movement, making art, or travelling the world? Of course, the ancient philosophers had long discussions about the relationship between practical philosophy and theoretical philosophy. At times, they even discussed practical action versus theoretical study (in some sense, that is the subtext of most Platonic dialogues).

Here's a telling short tale from the Jewish rabbinic sages. The story is set in Lod, a centre for study particularly in the period between the Romans' destruction of the Second Jerusalem Temple in 70 CE and Hadrian's persecution of 135 CE. In this period, many laws associated with temple service and political authority were abrogated, and the rabbinic sages were emerging as the leaders of the dominant group of surviving Jews.

The story is set in the attic of a person's house, often the gathering place of scholars and courts, a semipublic place not directly in the public square. In a city with study houses, in a time without political sovereignty, a discussion arises in an attic room about the role of study.

The passage bears two or even three readings.

> Rabbi Tarfon and the elders were reclining in the upper story of Nitzah's house in Lod when this question was raised before them: Is study greater or is practice greater? Rabbi Tarfon answered, saying practice is greater. Rabbi Akiva answered, saying study is greater. They all then answered, saying that study is greater because study leads to practice.[2]

Such a text requires careful study. The first step is noticing the interior structure of the passage. There's a question with three answers. The question seems to be about the comparative worth of theory and praxis, of thinking and of doing. The answers point, at first, in opposing directions: Tarfon believes actions are most important, that one must do, not merely think. But Akiva responds that whatever value there is in the doing, study is more valuable. The solution, as it were, cited in the name of consensus, qualifies Akiva's response. Yes, study is greater, but only because it will, in turn, lead to practice.

Here is an ethical justification for study: the value of study is not more for its own sake but because it will have an impact. Study will, in fact, transform our practice.

Translated to today, we would not say simply that university education is a better choice than getting on with it, than leading your life. We would claim that a university education will enhance or even redirect your life and what you will do. We might say that the kinds of thinking you'll learn to do in a research university will open paths in the world of action. We might even say that a university education will guide you into the labour market while changing society and its decisions. This broader impact of study – beyond individual priorities – drives society's demand for institutions that provide university education.

This Talmudic text requires a second reading. Who are these particular rabbis? What are they studying? And where, specifically, is this argument occurring? The participants and the location indicate that the original discussion was taking place in the early second century CE, either during or close in time to the persecution of Judaism. During that persecution, Romans decreed death for practising and teaching Judaism. (Akiva would eventually die for teaching.) The subject of this debate is the commandments, laws, and traditions of the Torah. Should they be taught or practised even at the risk of one's life? At the moment the sages meet in the house, the vital question they're considering is the survival of Judaism.

Akiva was born in Lod, Tarfon was the leading rabbinic teacher in Lod, and both men were key figures in the rabbinic movement. These early sages were meeting in someone's house partly because it was a safe place to hold the debate. In other texts, this house is the location of critical arguments on whether one must first study or first practice and on which commandments must not be transgressed even at the expense of one's life.[3]

The passage continues with a third sage, Rabbi Yosi of Galilee, arguing that study is greater than practice. He points out that many commandments and laws were given long before they could be practised, since the Bible presents the entire body of laws as having been given to Moses while the Israelites were still in the desert (around 1000 BCE), after their exodus from Egypt.

Sometimes study is possible for the sake of a future practice impossible in one's own time. Again, the meaning of *study* includes a relation with the future linked to what students and the students' students will learn and do. "Leading to practice" is a kind of history of the future. In the context of persecution, when the land is not properly settled and the Temple is destroyed, Rabbi Yosi's argument reflects a sense that study will preserve the Jews until the time when practice can become possible again – a wish that gets displaced onto a messianic future in the face of Roman hegemony.

In this second reading, study has an urgency, a strange existential urgency, pertaining to how to survive when the practice of the law is no longer possible and not yet possible. Study is not simply for the sake of knowledge but to prepare for the future because the action of study is the more worthy act. The Jews' zeal for study is not disinterested: it is a kind of interruption in the press of the present time. It is a vital interruption more valuable for the future than simply acting.

A third reading resituates the text yet again. Jewish texts are often commentaries, and this story was itself cited to comment on an earlier text. How does it work as a commentary? Editing landed this story from the second century CE into a fifth-century compilation, the *Babylonian*

Talmud, where it reads as a commentary on the Mishnah, the early third-century foundational text of Jewish law. The story appears in the interpretation of the following text: "He who is versed in Bible, Mishnah, and the way of the world will not hurry to sin, for it is said 'a threefold cord is not quickly broken.' (Eccl. 4.12) But he who lacks Bible, Mishnah and the way of the world does not belong to civilisation."[4]

The question of this Mishnah is the value of study. In a world now removed from the persecutions, from the temptation of revolt, and from the likelihood of a quick restoration of a society fit for practising all biblical law, the authors of the Mishnah – the students of the students of the group meeting in that house – choose to justify study. They stipulate that both the Bible and Mishnah must be studied. One requires engagement with the traditional text (the Bible) and with the more contemporary one (the Mishnah) because, for both theoretical and practical matters, the contemporary one offers a vital connection to the current situation.

Study is not merely historical. Indeed, there's reciprocal interrogation, as even in this text, the biblical quotation from Ecclesiastes is brought to reflect on the value of study. The word *Mishnah* means "repetition"; one needs to learn the original and its repetition. The word *Talmud*, moreover, means "study." More than two centuries later, the Talmudic text (500 CE) still cites the story from the time of persecution (130 CE) to comment on the middle text (200 CE) about how study itself is good. Removed from the urgency of the original debate, the citation of that debate reaffirms that the questions about study are vital.

In a world where practice is no longer part of the debate, the theory that study is greater requires some disturbance, which Rabbi Tarfon injects. The memory of the urgent discussion now challenges the ongoing stable practice of studying and comments on (and questions) the moralizing view that study will keep one from sin, and prevent one from becoming wicked. Instead, we have an argument at Nitzah's house – a contest between the sages who stabilized the world of study and the later sages who cite the argument. When the world has settled around a text and established study practices, a sense of urgency and passionate concern for the future becomes especially valuable.

Such is the logic, also, of the university and its history. Our questions about research universities in the present do not have the same urgency as those in the past (and this sense of urgency is not the same in all places in our time). Universities in many countries beyond Canada have faced challenges in the past decades. As I write, many are facing severe challenges today. The university's own past can serve as moralizing rhetoric for how good the university is for students or the world – universities make people better. Student engagement is similarly complex. Some students study for a moral direction, some study to survive, and some study to negotiate their own relationship with their past. All of these relationships are illuminated by recognizing that study is balanced with doing, with practice, in a living tension.

Today, students come to the research university, and they choose to study. Indeed, in Canada's public system, students work in order to come to university. Some will say they are simply looking for a better job, but the research university provides a higher education; a university education is not simply a bureaucratic exercise such as a career-development service (you can sign up with companies that can provide that service).

But how is the university, as a place, suitable for study? Is the university like Nitzah's house in Lod?

When exploring the idea of discord, I referred to the risks of terror – of silencing those suffering wrongs. The rabbis in Nitzah's house faced mortal danger but continued the argument in a safe place. Several, including Akiva, were martyred. Later, in safer times, the scholars recalled the need for a safe place in times of danger. Whether we see our times as safer or as burgeoning with danger, the safe place is one where we can struggle to listen to others, to find ways to register and address suffering, current and past. In a complex society, with much promise and much injustice, the university can offer a safe place, not by providing settled knowledge but by engaging in critique and inquiry to find new ways of addressing the world.

The study places in the university are, for the most part, familiar: the lecture hall, the seminar classroom, the laboratory, and the library. We've visited these places earlier in this book – especially in the discussion of PhD education. One could imagine that students "show up" because they "have to." The rabbis also said, "It is not hearing the lecture but the running to it." So long as the lecture hall is restricted to providing information, to teaching knowledge that is settled, then its role in university education will be diminished, and it may not serve the university in the long run.

Students do come to the lectures, but they can also stream them, in real time or as a recording. If lectures are only for information, then streaming great lecturers from other universities might do the trick. Indeed, great lectures are very much about making information interesting. They verge on entertainment.

But the lecture hall is also a place for learning to question, to reflect, to challenge settled knowledge, even that of the professor. Perhaps because they challenge students in that face-to-face moment, the truly great lecturers are not mere entertainers. The excitement of the question, of studying, trumps the acquisition of knowledge and the pleasure of being a mere spectator. It is not clear how much longer the large lecture hall can survive – its future will depend on the interactions and immediacy of the challenge the professor delivers and the challenges the professor welcomes from students.

In contrast, the seminar classroom is uniquely suited to listening to one another and learning how to listen and think in response. Whether the teacher is a graduate student or a professor, there's an intrinsic value in showing up. The seminar is a place where new ideas are tried out and new questions are heard. One learns from another's questions, and one learns about oneself by speaking and listening. An online chat room or virtual room struggles to host this back-and-forth, side-by-side interaction. Intellectual alliances and rifts generate much of the experience of learning, and the level of questioning pushes each person to reflect on their own position, in the room and in the world. There is more to reflect on when students are residents in the city.

One might think that laboratories are primarily a place where people make things and do things – but that would make them factories. Rather, so much of education (especially teaching students how to do research and how to inquire) depends on being in the lab. The pandemic closures were especially disruptive to this kind of study. The lab's mixture of tasks, reflection, conversation, review, group meetings, and one-to-one conversations makes it a remarkable place to learn. Being in the lab is not optional. The ability to inquire, to frame hypotheses, to generate experiments, analyze data, and write it all up – all these aspects of study depend on regular attendance in the lab. For scientists who go on to research in government or industrial labs, labs are not simply training; they inculcate habits of study that continue in their research lives. For students who end up professors teaching in research universities, labs are places where they learn how to teach others how to conduct research (how to study in this laboratory manner).

Students come to the university lab because they want to learn with others; indeed, they want to learn how to learn with others, to learn how to discover new knowledge. When someone "only wants to get a job," the lab will either elicit their desire to learn and attend to others or they will not succeed. Engagement with study is what makes a person valuable in the job market. Being addicted to study, to learning new things, can be amplified and taught in a research university.

Lastly, most humanities students (and a good many others) go to the library to study. The popularity of the library came as a welcome surprise as universities shrank their book collections – discarding some, storing others, limiting new acquisitions, and digitizing. The cause was quite simple: most students read online. For journals, only historical and small-circulation volumes require paper copies. As for books and anthologies, while some historical archives and foreign-language volumes might still be inaccessible, many of these, including rarer books and even manuscripts, will become available online in the coming years.

And yet students still stream into the libraries. Many campuses have devoted significant funds to expanding and refurbishing their libraries. Libraries have been renovated to host studying, and the most important zones are now the study spaces. Students come to study alone but also to study with others in small groups. They come to study in an online environment, multitasking with TikTok, Snapchat, discussion boards, email, and other windows open, all while sitting at a desk or in a comfortable chair in the library. Somehow, studying seems more "at home" in the library than sitting at home or in a coffee shop.

Making the most of this trend is a challenge for research universities. New library spaces are built, money is raised, chairs are filled. In the demographic game of getting students to show up and fill seats, the library is a great leader. But what does this mean? Again, there are parallels with the laboratory, but the library is optional and seems, for students, to have paramount desirability. Here we have a place of intellectual freedom and sociality. The library is unregulated (aside from limits on food and noise) and reserved for students. The library is the very heart of university study – even more so than classrooms. As such, it represents the dignity of study. One used to say the library had a single purpose – to read books. Now libraries house many activities, all of which are linked and constitute study. The library dignifies conversations, work groups, and solitary readers. It's a refuge from lectures and classes, a place to stop and linger, to focus.

Unlike classes, which are on the clock, the library is in some ways off the clock. And there's been a steady push to extend the hours. The library is for time that is not spent commuting, working, or in class. It is the real time of study. Students are there to write papers, do homework, and prepare for class by reading or doing problem sets or exercises. They're there to talk with others about the work they need to do for their classes and about other people's assignments. This education-bound set of tasks bleeds into all of their conversations in real and virtual space.

But – and this is my point – the library is a real place that draws students, however born-digital or online their sense of existence may be. Of course, libraries need Wi-Fi, and books are still in circulation. Most journals are available and sometimes read in paper copies – but beyond changes in information technology, the library has reasserted its role as the place for study.

Universities for Our World

The research university is a place where students congregate to study. The students' commute links the civic places (where the students live) with study spaces in the university. There are many institutions and social practices that preserve, transmit, and renew knowledge outside the university. Our students live amid them. Toronto, like many other cities, is an immigrant city. Students come from diverse cultures. They include people who have moved from different corners of the world and First Nations peoples who preceded settlers and immigrants and on whose territory the university resides. Students come with many languages, religions, ethnicities, and histories. Recently, there has been a vast expansion of international students, who are more likely to return to their home countries following their education.

The university acts as a safe house for the most profound questioning of traditions, for questioning the empires and hegemonic orders of our time. Questions about language, history, science, values, gender, sexuality, religion, or politics that might not be cultivated in the home community, or in the local metropolitan area, or in localities far away, are explored and developed in the research university. Students enjoy a sense of freedom to entertain hard questions, to revise the history of their city, of Canada, of a specific immigrant community, or of the world. They occupy a space where such reflection is authorized and social pressure is mediated and limited. They are not simply learning to think for themselves but learning to think in response to others and learning to learn with others.

The university can be a place that knits civil society more closely together. Critical study is, indeed, part of learning how to live with great differences and great resources from other communities. In exchange, the questions that reside in a complex civil society can produce a unique mode of research.

Other institutions are negotiating the weave of civil society. Social interactions should provide a fundamental opportunity to participate safely and avoid what Lyotard called "terror" – the risk of being banished or silenced. Theatre and performance provide this kind of a safe space, as does the courtroom. In both, conflicts are staged or constructed. Antagonism is respected and sustained with rules and clear limitations on what can be said or done to the other party.

In the classroom, the "loser," the person whose viewpoint is subjected to critique, loses some honour but remains a member of the class. A hypothesis that is refuted by data is important for learning how to do research.

We can compare the multiplicity of viewpoints in the classroom with the legislature. The house is self-regulating and committed to preserving room for minority parties and room for debate. The defeated party is neither exiled nor imprisoned but remains seated. While the court operates with the threat of coercion in criminal cases, the legislature is constituted to sustain the losing party.

The university is self-regulating, but it does not merely tolerate multiplicity – it recruits, encourages, and engages with it. Knowledge discovered at a research university indirectly affects policies and may also transform culture, business, religion, and all aspects of society. The university is not, however, the place where laws are made, nor is it the place where verdicts of personal liability are announced.

What these comparisons indicate is that much of society is organized around practices of institutionalized conflict and tension. The idea of discord and the idea of responsibility animate many institutions. There are resolutions, in some cases, but they are only temporary. The common goal is to create a forum where debate can happen, where different sides have a chance to speak. The idea of discord is vital for civil society, for living constructively with diversity.

An urban epistemology locates university spaces in the larger context of society while the idea of permeability guides us to position students as the key link between universities and society. Students pass through the university almost daily. Commuting creates a research university intellectually engaged with diverse students from across the region. As such, it's capable of engaging diverse communities. If we can imagine the university's research impact in terms of the tens of thousands of students who learn how to research, then we can also imagine the university's educational impact not only on students but also on the whole city, on its institutions, and in the communities where students live. The university is in fact working on one of our great challenges: How can we live together? The urban university binds university education (both research and critical reflection) closely with diverse communities and sources of knowledge in the city. The flow of students generates dialogues and exchanges that can educate a whole urban region, tapping our capacities to listen and discern new insights.

Conclusion
A Future University

The philosophical reflections that appear in these pages often take a historical turn to focus on the future of the research university. Philosophers often think about things in unsettling, unexpected ways to generate new ways of looking at things, and recourse to new ideas helps recast the demands upon our universities and the changes underway to meet them.

Within any university, the agents of change are various. Today, much of the heavy lifting has fallen to a new stream of teaching professors who bear less responsibility for generating new research but have time and again shown passion and creativity for teaching the logic of inquiry. Alternative academics, who often hold PhDs, are working in the offices of deans and vice-presidents, with provosts and presidents to encourage others to transform curriculums; connect with the city and local communities; and facilitate studying across schools, disciplines, and faculties, all to create new opportunities for students to learn the logic of inquiry (inside out, round and round, and upside down). I don't mean to exclude research professors or even presidents and deans – some set excellent priorities and struggle to find the resources and incentives to effect change.

Of course, the most important agents are the students. Given a place at the table, these temporary members of the university often prove not only eloquent but also engaged, reflective, and, frankly, inspiring. Their eagerness to learn and to create new knowledge is a rich resource for the renewal of universities. When we recognize that the students are the key link between universities and diverse urban communities, we'll be more likely to welcome them to the table.

Let's return to my reflections on space – the idea of an urban epistemology. The research university is a place where students congregate to study. The university plays a vital role in strengthening civil society by fostering critical study and engagement with diverse perspectives. Learning isn't just about acquiring knowledge – it's also about understanding and navigating differences while drawing from the rich resources of other communities. I called this a "society with questions" rather than a knowledge economy because the university's mission is not just to transfer existing knowledge but to cultivate inquisitive minds that seek new insights. In an open-ended future, the university helps keep possibilities alive.

In exchange, the questions that live in civil society can produce a unique mode of research. These questions animate the professions – in health care, social services, politics, business, engineering, education, information technology, and more. Other questions – about the future of the earth and the beings that live on it, about energy and time – are the stuff of the natural and biological sciences. Perhaps most demanding are questions about society itself – about our diverse traditions and histories, about the realities of immigration and displacement, about gender and sexuality, about the legacies of past injustice, and about how we'll manage to live together in the future.

Research universities teach students how to listen to others. University education can have indirect effects, but the main goal is to learn how to learn with others and to learn to think in response to others' questions. The university provides a safe space for engaging with inflammatory and difficult perspectives, with questions from the past that disturb our comfort in the present, with demands for change that disrupt the present situation. Freed from terror and the need to punish wrong opinions, the university can engage with conflicts and meet calls from society with greater openness. It can challenge the student to learn difficult knowledge.

And when the student goes home, he can engage with his own communities, with family, friends, community leaders, same-age peers, and so on. In contrast to the safe space of the university, much is on the line. Social forces are alive and in play. Conflict may come at a cost, but it may also lead to renewal and change. The student is a medium of exchange. She must balance the claims of her social world with the freedom of inquiry she experiences in the university. She'll hear questions at home that her professors don't ask, and then she'll get on the bus or the subway and commute back to the university for another class and study break in the library before heading off to work.

Many countries like Canada have very high rates of postsecondary education. By involving the entire city, its institutions, and the communities where students live – the university becomes an active force in addressing one of our biggest challenges: How can we live together? The urban university connects university education (both research and critical reflection) more deeply with the diverse societies and sources of knowledge of the city.

Let me conclude by turning again to the theme of time. The students who flow in and out of campus are temporary members of the university – they study, complete their degrees, and then take up careers, professions, and vocations in the world. "Time to completion" is a metric that matters, particularly when the university bears heavy costs in relation to housing and vast extracurricular activities. But that's not what I mean when I talk about time.

On the contrary, the central topic of this book is what kind of thinking, what kind of education, is suited to our times – to the future bearing down on us with a series of challenges and needs. Building on Hermann Cohen and much of twentieth-century philosophy, I prioritize the future as the primary aspect of time and distinguish inquiry from critique and knowledge – emphasizing the need to generate new insights rather than merely analyzing or preserving what we already know. I do not discount other kinds of postsecondary education (such as vocational colleges, formation in the liberal arts, or critical thinking).

But in the case of the research university, time is, most of all, about the future. At the research university, students flow in and out to take up new roles in society, and the university has a distinct responsibility to teach them how to become the creators of that future. Study can lead to a more rigorous and more creative view of the world than the one in which they were raised and upon which they can improve. The best justification for the research university as an institution – one that persists even as it grows and changes, along with the many people who spend their whole adult lives in it – is the education it provides. It's the students who learn the logic of inquiry so they can chart new courses into the future. A new kind of university is taking shape – one that empowers students to recognize the questions that will shape our future. By cultivating rigorous inquiry and creative thinking, it will equip them to generate new insights, expand knowledge, and forge new ways of living together.

Acknowledgments

The genesis of this book was complex and protracted, and I have debts that exceed those I can only briefly note here. I will start at the end, with my amazing and creative editors at On Campus/UBC Press, Lesley Erickson, Nadine Pedersen, Katrina Petrik, and Melissa Pitts. With their efforts, a work written by a philosopher for philosophers has become a book that can offer thoughts to a much wider public.

While I had presented earlier thoughts and versions of the ideas discussed here at numerous universities, the turning point for this book was the opportunity to deliver the John V. Clyne Lectures under the auspices of Green College at the University of British Columbia in 2019. Principal Mark Vessey hosted me as a visiting fellow, and I engaged in many dialogues and learned a great deal from the discussions about the lectures and from many other conversations.

Thank you from the bottom of my heart to my friends and colleagues who had extensive conversations with me, shared in workshops, and in many cases, have read various drafts as this book came into being: Carl Amrhein, Ian Angus, Gage Averill, John Borrows, Keith Brown, Rachel Brown, Jonathan Crane, Angela Esterhammer, George Fallis, David Ford, Samir Gandesha, Meric Gertler, Vivek Goel, Simon Goldhill, Paul Gooch, Anthony Grafton, Michael Higton, Timothy Jenkins, Glen Jones, Claire Katz, Greg Kelly, Premesh Lalu, Susan McCahan, Tracey McIntosh, Will Robbins, Geoffrey Rockwell, Alessandro Schiesaro, Brian Cantwell Smith, Stephen Toope, Ian Wei, Ira Wells, Kathleen Woodward, and Paul Yachnin.

To the many others who asked questions and encouraged me, great thanks. All errors of fact or of judgment are my own.

The Jackman Humanities Institute at the University of Toronto is the original context of this project. I was honoured to be its inaugural director and to have received much encouragement from Hal and Maruja Jackman. They have been not only generous donors, but also true supporters of the university.

My daughters, Ariel and Robin, and Deirdre, who has been my partner for the whole ride with this book, have listened to these matters far beyond the call of duty and offered loving patience and encouragement. And I would add that my parents, Z"L, helped me in many ways – by valuing university education and, in my father's case, by pointing out to me that my own earlier work in Jewish philosophy is richly connected to my ideas about universities.

The 130 students I taught in a series of courses on universities have pride of place for their influence and effect on my thinking: to them I offer many thanks. It has been my great privilege to learn for them, from them, and best of all, with them, just what sort of task the university has if it wants to make a great difference in our world. Students are not only the topic of this book, but also its goal and my tutors.

Philosophers' Biographies

Hermann Cohen (1842–1918). A philosopher who pioneered the return to Kant's philosophy, with its critical edge, after the Idealists, hence the label "neo-Kantian," leading to the Marburg School. He was a rare Jewish professor in the university world and wrote about Jewish philosophical themes throughout his career. He had a wide influence on the philosophy of science, socialist politics, Jewish thought, and the Frankfurt School. Rosenzweig was one of his students. Cohen was cast into oblivion by the rise of the Nazi state and was largely ignored in the history of philosophy.

J.G. Fichte (1762–1814). A German Idealist philosopher who transformed Kant's philosophy and offered a radical interpretation of subjectivity and the pure I.

Wilhelm von Humboldt (1767–1835). A man of letters and a pioneer in the field of linguistics. He was one of the great humanists of his time, successful as a civil servant and adviser and largely responsible for the founding of the University of Berlin.

Immanuel Kant (1724–1804). The central figure of modern philosophy, Kant developed rigorous critical reflection on the capacity of human reason to know metaphysical truths. He was a champion of the Enlightenment and was subject to censorship for his rationalist religious views.

He initiated a Copernican revolution in philosophy, arguing that human reason provided the order that made the sciences possible. In moral thought, he championed autonomy, the idea that each person should give the moral law to him- or herself.

Emmanuel Levinas (1906–95). Levinas was a leader in Jewish philosophy and a French philosopher who helped introduce the school of phenomenology to France. Originally from Lithuania, he was a student of Husserl and Heidegger. While interned in a hard labour camp during the Second World War, his Lithuanian family was murdered by the Nazis. His wife and daughter, hidden in a convent in the south of France, survived. After the war, he continued as a teacher and then as the principal of a teacher-training school in Paris. After publishing his main book, *Totality and Infinity*, in 1961, he finally became a professor and concluded his career at the Sorbonne. He continued his role in the Jewish intellectual community and offered commentaries on Talmudic texts.

Jean-François Lyotard (1924–98). Lyotard was a French philosopher most famous for articulating postmodernism. His path was complex and included Marxism, theories of desire, phenomenology, and political critique. He argued that the master narratives of progress were no longer binding in the late twentieth century. His most important work, *The Differend*, explores the limits of language and the responsibility to attend to things that exceed the current protocols of evidence, such as the Holocaust and the challenge of proving charges of genocide.

Franz Rosenzweig (1886–1929). Rosenzweig was a leader of the Jewish Renaissance in Germany in the 1920s. His dissertation on Hegel qualified him for a university position, but he declined it and founded an adult education program in Frankfurt. His main text, *The Star of Redemption*, argues for the rich interplay of philosophy, theology, Christianity, and Judaism in the living task of redeeming the world. Stricken with ALS, he was paralyzed but continued to write and meet with people until his death in 1929. He and Martin Buber translated the Hebrew Bible into German. The result is a stunning and important work of translation.

F.W.J. Schelling (1775–1854). Schelling was a German Idealist philosopher whose career went through several key phases and influenced several waves of thought – most importantly, Idealism, leading up to Hegel, and then, later, his philosophy of existence, which directly led to a rich set of "existentialists," including Rosenzweig and others.

Friedrich Schleiermacher (1768–1834). Schleiermacher was a theologian and philosopher. He developed a theory of religious experience that cast it as a feeling of absolute dependence. He also translated Plato's dialogues into German and made a key contribution to the philosophy of language by developing the field of hermeneutics (the science of interpretation). He was a member of the Berlin Academy and the provost of the University of Berlin.

Notes

Introduction

1 Christopher Newfield, *The Great Mistake: How We Wrecked Public Universities and How We Can Fix Them* (Johns Hopkins University Press, 2016).
2 Ronald Barnett, ed., *The Future University: Ideas and Possibilities* (Routledge, 2012).
3 John Henry Newman, *The Idea of a University* (University of Notre Dame Press, 1982).

Chapter 1: Teaching Undergraduates to Do Research

1 Friedrich Schleiermacher, *Gelegentliche Gedanken über Universitäten in deutschem Sinn: Nebst einem Anhang über eine neu zu errichtende* (G. Reimer, 1808), published in English as *Occasional Thoughts on Universities in the German Sense: With an Appendix Regarding a University Soon to Be Established*, translated by Terrence N. Tice and Edwina Lawler (EM Text, 1991).
2 Schleiermacher, *Occasional Thoughts*, 16–17.
3 Hermann Cohen, *Logik der reinen Erkenntnis* [The logic of pure cognition] (Georg Olms Verlag, 1977), 154–55 (my translation).
4 Cohen, *Logik der reinen Erkenntnis*, 429–30 (my translation).
5 Cohen, *Logik der reinen Erkenntnis*, 523–24.
6 Schleiermacher, *Occasional Thoughts*, 21.
7 Wilhelm von Humboldt, "Über die innere und äussere Organisation der höheren wissenschaftlichen Anstalten in Berlin," *Gesammelte Schriften*, Herausgegeben von der Königlich Preussischen Akademie der Wissenschaften (B. Behr's Verlag, 1903), 250–60, published in English as "On the Spirit and the Organisational Framework of Intellectual Institutions in Berlin," translated by Edward Shils, *Minerva* 8, 2 (1970): 247.
8 Humboldt, "On the Spirit and the Organisational Framework," 243.

Chapter 2: Multiplying Inquiry and Innovation Beyond the University

1 Emmanuel Levinas, *Totalité et infini: Essai sur l'extériorité* [Totality and infinity: An essay on exteriority] (Martinus Nijhoff, 1971), 254 (my translation).
2 Emmanuel Levinas, "Le pacte," in *L'au-delà du verset* (Les Éditions de Minuit, 1982), 87–106. Published in English in *Beyond the Verse*, translated by Gary D. Mole (Indiana University Press, 1994).
3 Levinas, "Le pacte," 105 (my translation).
4 Levinas, "Le pacte," 105–6 (my translation).
5 Levinas, "Le pacte," 106 (my translation).

Chapter 3: Slowing Down Reading and Thinking in the Digital Age

An earlier version of this chapter was originally published in *College Literature* 42, 2 (2015): 241–79, copyright © 2015 Johns Hopkins University Press and West Chester University of Pennsylvania.

1 Brian Cantwell Smith, *The Promise of Artificial Intelligence: Reckoning and Judgment* (MIT Press, 2019).
2 Jean-François Lytoard, *La condition postmoderne: Rapport sur le savoir* (Les Éditions de Minuit, 1979), published in English as *The Postmodern Condition: A Report on Knowledge*, translated by Geoff Bennington and Brian Massumi (University of Minnesota Press, 1984).
3 Lyotard, *The Postmodern Condition*, 32–33.
4 Lytoard, *The Postmodern Condition*, 42.
5 Jean-François Lyotard, *Le différend* (Les Éditions de Minuit, 1983), published in English as *The Differend: Phrases in Dispute*, translated by George Van Den Abbeele (University of Minnesota Press, 1988).
6 Lyotard, *The Differend*, 20–21.
7 See David F. Ford and C.C. Pecknold, ed., *The Promise of Scriptural Reasoning* (Blackwell, 2006).

Chapter 4: Thinking Like a Professional and Responding to Society's Questions

1 Immanuel Kant, *Der Streit der Fakultäten* (1798), published in a facing-page, bilingual edition as *The Conflict of the Faculties*, translated by Mary J. Gregor (University of Nebraska Press, 1979).
2 Franz Rosenzweig, *Franz Rosenzweig: Der Mensch und sein Werk: Gesammelte Schriften*, vol. 2, *Der Stern der Erlösung* (Nijhoff, 1976), published in English as *The Star of Redemption*, translated by Barbara E. Galli (University of Wisconsin Press, 2005).
3 Franz Rosenzweig, "Letter to Friedrich Meinecke, 30 August 1920," in *Franz Rosenzweig: Der Mensch und sein Werk: Gesammelte Schriften*, vol. 1, *Briefe und Tagebücher* (Nijhoff, 1979) s. 681, published in English, in part, as *Franz Rosenzweig: His Life and Thoughts*, translated by Francis C. Golffing, presented by Nahum N. Glatzer (Shocken, 1953), 94–98. Translation adjusted by the author.

4 Rosenzweig, "Letter to Friedrich Meinecke, 30 August 1920," s. 681.
5 Rosenzweig, *Franz Rosenzweig: His Life and Thoughts*, s. 681.

Chapter 5: Connecting Universities to Cities and Communities

1 Schleiermacher, "On University Customs and Control," in *Occasional Thoughts*, 49–60.
2 *Babylonian Talmud*, Kiddushin 40b.
3 *Talmud Yerushalmi*, Pesahim 30b; and *Babylonian Talmud*, Sanhedrin 74a.
4 *Mishnah*, Kiddushin I:10.

Index

Note: "(i)" after a page number indicates an illustration or configuration diagram; "(t)" after a page number indicates a table.

Printed and bound in Canada

Set in Calibri, Sabon, and Times New Roman
by Artegraphica Design Co.

Editor: Lesley Erickson

Proofreader and indexer: Cheryl Lemmens

Cover designer: Will Brown

Illustration credits:
(1) Architas, Wikimedia Commons (CC BY-SA 4.0);
(2)–(5) Courtesy of the Thomas Fisher Rare Book Library,
University of Toronto

Authorized Representative:
Easy Access System Europe –
Mustamäe tee 50, 10621 Tallinn, Estonia,
gpsr.requests@easproject.com